Finding Grace

The Inspiring True Story of Therapy Dogs
Bringing Comfort, Hope & Love to a Hurting World

finding
grace

**Larry Randolph &
Jennifer Marshall Bleakley**

TYNDALE
MOMENTUM®

A Tyndale nonfiction imprint

Visit Tyndale online at tyndale.com.

Visit Tyndale Momentum online at tyndalemomentum.com.

Check out Canines for Christ at k9forchrist.org.

Tyndale, Tyndale's quill logo, *Tyndale Momentum*, and the Tyndale Momentum logo are registered trademarks of Tyndale House Ministries. Tyndale Momentum is a nonfiction imprint of Tyndale House Publishers, Carol Stream, Illinois.

Finding Grace: The Inspiring True Story of Therapy Dogs Bringing Comfort, Hope, and Love to a Hurting World

Designed by Libby Dykstra

Published in association with the literary agency, WTA Media LLC, Franklin, TN.

For information about special discounts for bulk purchases, please contact Tyndale House Publishers at csresponse@tyndale.com, or call 1-855-277-9400.

Library of Congress Cataloging-in-Publication Data

A catalog record for this book is available from the Library of Congress.

ISBN 978-1-4964-7360-8 SC

Printed in the United States of America

29	28	27	26	25	24	23
7	6	5	4	3	2	1

I dedicate this book to my dear, sweet mother, who
set the foundation for my relationship with God
and who helped define who I am today.

LARRY RANDOLPH

For Gracie Randolph and Gracie Bleakley—and all the dogs
who point people's hearts to the unconditional love of God.

JENNIFER MARSHALL BLEAKLEY

Prologue

"WE'RE HOME NOW, GRACIE," Larry said soothingly to his three-year-old white Lab. "You can relax."

Gracie's rib cage heaved rapidly. She had been panting since Larry and his wife, Susan, picked her up from the pet-sitter's house. After spending ten days away from her favorite humans, who had vacationed in the Caribbean, Gracie had no intention of letting either of them out of her sight. She leaned her full eighty pounds against Larry's leg, while keeping her eyes fixed on Susan.

Larry gently pushed on Gracie's right side to encourage her to lie down. It was a move he and Gracie had practiced countless times so that lonely, hurting people could pet the gentle dog. As always, Gracie eagerly complied, exposing her fuzzy white belly and casting a forlorn look at Susan.

"All right, all right," Susan said, surrendering to the unspoken plea and rubbing Gracie's coarse white fur. The dog inhaled deeply, then released a contented sigh. A few minutes later, her breathing slowed to a normal rhythm.

After giving Gracie a few more brisk belly rubs, Susan stood up. "I'm going to take a shower and finish unpacking." She kissed Larry's forehead, ruffled his salt-and-pepper hair, and headed for the bedroom.

Gracie sat up and Larry gave her a final scratch, then grabbed the remote and sank comfortably on the sofa. Their trip to Saint Bart's for Susan's sixtieth birthday had been wonderful—and so very needed after a hectic season with their ever-growing therapy dog ministry—but there really was no place like home.

Gracie padded over to her favorite spot—a mat in front of the sliding glass doors where she could see both the bedroom door and the sofa. She circled three times, lay down, rested her head between her paws, and closed her eyes for a much-deserved nap.

Larry flipped through the channels until he found a golf game, stretched out his legs, and leaned his head back against the soft cushion. The gentle cadence of the commentator's voice quickly worked its magic, and Larry began to doze off.

Moments later, he was jolted awake by an uncharacteristic growl. Gracie was racing toward the bedroom.

"Gracie?" Larry quickly got up and followed her. She was standing in front of the closed bathroom door, barking. But her bark sounded different than he had ever heard it before.

It was deeper.

Throatier.

Frantic.

Larry couldn't hear any water running in the bathroom. Gracie continued barking. *Surely Susan would have come out to see what all the ruckus was about.* Something was wrong.

Panic welling up inside him, he knocked on the bathroom door. "Susan?" He paused for a second. Gracie pawed wildly at the rug in front of the door as though she was trying to tunnel under it.

"Susan?" Larry called louder, then pushed the door open.

Susan was unconscious on the bathroom floor.

CHAPTER ONE

FOUR YEARS EARLIER

Larry eased the door closed behind him and treaded softly down the hall. He smiled to himself, thinking of how quietly he used to sneak from the bedroom, afraid any noise would wake his new wife. But after nearly five years of marriage, Larry had come to realize that Susan could sleep through almost anything.

Sunrise was still thirty minutes away, and there was no light streaming through the windows. Larry made a pot of coffee in the kitchen, poured himself a mug, then continued to the living room. His routine was as familiar as it was necessary. He craved these quiet moments in the morning before the noise of his workday began. It was a routine he had put into practice years ago when nothing had felt familiar or certain, and his soul had been desperate to hold on to something solid.

Placing his mug on the side table, he settled into his recliner and reached for his Bible.

"Good morning, Lord," he prayed aloud. "Thank you for this new day and for being here with me."

The hum of the air conditioner and overhead fan—necessities for enduring Florida summers—provided a soothing soundtrack as Larry sat in quiet awareness of God's presence. With a busy day ahead of him, this focused time was like fuel for his heart and mind. He prayed first for Susan. Then for his daughters, Kristy and Heather; Susan's daughters, Tara and Brooke; their sons-in-law; and his young grandchildren. His prayers then turned to friends from their Bible study and for his workday ahead, full of real estate proposals and scheduled client meetings.

"Lord, I give my day to you. Help me speak with wisdom and grace today. Guide my conversations and help others see you in me."

As he opened his Bible to the passage he had been reading the day before, an odd restlessness settled over him. It was a feeling he had experienced several times over the last few weeks. Thankfully, though, the feeling never lingered. He figured it was probably work-related stress. *Or maybe*, Larry thought, looking around the freshly painted living room, *this feeling has to do with Susan's determination to repaint every room in our town house.*

No one could accuse his wife of taking it easy in her early retirement. Instead, she poured herself into all the things she'd never had time for when she was working. Now Susan was busier than ever with her community Bible study, volunteering with Meals on Wheels, and turning their town house into a cozy and beautiful home. She joked that retirement had become a full-time job.

Larry took a sip of coffee and tried to push the unsettled feelings aside. After all, life was good. His own retirement was approaching, and he and Susan were looking forward to traveling and visiting their children and grandchildren. He had everything he'd ever wanted—everything that at one point in his life he'd thought he would never have again. Larry smiled to himself. *I'm sure my restless feelings are because I never know what color the living room will be when I come home.*

His Bible was open to the third chapter of Proverbs. Even though he had read through the book countless times, there was always some new nugget of wisdom God would show him.

He started reading silently, then paused at Proverbs 3:3: "Let love and faithfulness never leave you; bind them around your neck, write them on the tablet of your heart."

"God, please help me to pursue love and faithfulness in all I do. Write them on my heart."

He stopped again two verses later—not to pray, but to catch his breath. His heart was racing. It wasn't alarming. In fact, it almost felt . . . joyful, like the anticipation before opening a gift. He read Proverbs 3:5-6 aloud: "Trust in the LORD with all your heart and lean not on your own understanding; in all your ways submit to him, and he will make your paths straight."

Larry knew the words by heart, and yet it was like he was reading them for the first time. He leaned back in his chair and closed his eyes. Experience had taught him that this feeling of joyful anticipation while reading Scripture was usually God's Spirit gently speaking to him.

"Lord, I want to trust you fully and submit to your will. Is there something you want me to do?"

And then suddenly, in the silence, there it was.

Therapy dogs.

Larry's heart skipped a beat. *Therapy dogs?* Where had *that* thought come from?

"God, was that you?"

He already knew the answer. His heart said yes, even as his mind struggled to understand.

What did therapy dogs have to do with anything? He was a real estate developer, not a dog breeder. Or a therapist.

I don't even have a dog.

And yet a certainty washed over him that he hadn't felt since his first date with Susan—when he knew she would be his wife one day.

"Therapy dogs," he said, testing the words out on his lips.

He got up and began to pace back and forth between the living room and the kitchen.

"Therapy dogs . . ." he repeated. "Trust in the Lord with all your heart. Don't lean on your own understanding. Hold on to love and faithfulness . . . therapy dogs."

It was like trying to create one image from two different puzzles. "Lord, please help me understand."

He considered waking Susan. But what would he say? "Good morning, sweetheart. What do you think about therapy dogs?" No, he needed to sit with this a little while. As he turned back toward the living room, a figure caught his eye—a ceramic figure of a Basset Hound painted to look like Gus, sitting on the floor by the patio door.

Gus.

The dog's name made Larry smile as memories flooded his mind.

Gus had come into Larry's life at a time when he really needed a friend—especially one who didn't know what a failure he was.

Of course, his friends and family told him that he wasn't at fault for the economic downturn that had affected market conditions.

"It's the ebb and flow of the market," well-meaning colleagues would say. "Real estate is a fickle beast."

"You'll figure something out," Chris, his then-wife of fifteen years, reassured him. His girls, Kristy and Heather, stood by him: "Dad, we love you no matter what."

But deep down, Larry couldn't help but feel like a failure. He had let people down. People who had trusted him with their money. Whose investments were soon to be turned over to a court-appointed receivership when he filed for bankruptcy. It was a choice he hadn't wanted to make, but it was the only one that would give his investors a chance—albeit a small chance—of getting some of their money back.

He was trying to stay positive even when he had to give up his beautiful office in downtown Charlotte and work out of their guest room. He tried to stay busy—he needed to stay busy. But he could feel depression settling over him like a heavy quilt, making it difficult to feign excitement for a birthday dinner his wife and daughters had planned for him the week before his bankruptcy court date.

"Dad!" twelve-year-old Heather called out. "We have a birthday surprise for you! Come into the family room."

Larry mustered every ounce of energy he could to rise from the chair in his makeshift office and trudge down the hall. Forcing a smile, he rounded the corner, but when he spotted a squirmy long-eared puppy in Heather's arms, his entire face erupted in sincere joy.

"Happy birthday!" Heather, Kristy, and Chris called out in unison.

Larry couldn't remember ever feeling so surprised. He hadn't asked for a puppy. He hadn't even *thought* about getting another dog since their Chihuahua, Chichi, had bitten Heather several years ago, and they had to rehome him.

"What in the world . . ." Larry said, marveling at the little black, brown, and white Basset Hound Heather placed in his arms. He'd never seen one of them in real life before—only in ads for Hush Puppies shoes.

"Who is this?" he laughed as the puppy licked his chin.

"His name is Gus!" Heather beamed. "We named him that because he looks like a Gus."

"The girls thought you could use a friend during the day," Chris explained. Her tone was kind, even though her eyes were distant. Given the heated argument they'd had over finances earlier that morning—one of dozens they'd had over the past several weeks—Larry appreciated her attempt to put on a good front for the girls.

"Mom and Heather found an ad in the paper," fourteen-year-old Kristy piped in. "Do you like him?"

Larry held Gus up to his face, searched his soulful, humanlike eyes—eyes whose depths seemed to hold both sorrow and hope—and found in them a kindred spirit.

"I think he's the most perfect dog I've ever seen," he said, planting a kiss on Gus's forehead. "And he's the best birthday present I've ever received. Thank you."

Larry set Gus on the floor, and the ten-pound puppy promptly tripped over his own ears.

"He's all feet and ears," Larry said with a laugh. He knelt down and set Gus back on his feet. "Don't worry, little guy. You'll grow into those ears."

Gus kept Larry busy and distracted the week leading up to his courthouse date. Larry took him for two walks a day—often carrying Gus home because the puppy would become too tired to walk another step on his short legs. Gus's ears dipped into his water bowl every time he took a drink, and he was determined to shake off every water droplet so Larry was constantly wiping down the kitchen cabinets, floor, and walls.

But when the bankruptcy court date finally came, Larry was overwhelmed with grief and disappointment. After signing the final papers, he left the courthouse and wept. For himself. For his investors. And for his future.

"God, what do I do now?" he silently prayed.

Defeated and dejected, he dreaded going home. The girls would still be at school, and with the way he and Chris had been arguing over everything, he feared facing her. *How long will it be till I'm back here signing divorce papers?* he wondered.

Fears about his future all but consumed Larry, but they dissipated the moment he arrived home and saw Gus.

"Come on, Gus," he said, clipping a red leash to the puppy's matching collar. "Let's go for a walk."

As the two set off down the neighborhood sidewalk, Gus sniffed every blade of grass and tried to greet every person they passed, his velvety brown ears dragging along the ground the entire way.

"I promise, little buddy, someday you *will* grow into those ears."

Over the next few years, Gus did grow into his ears. And Larry slowly began to build back his real estate connections. However, just as the economy took an upturn, Larry and Chris's marriage took a downturn. And despite their best efforts at reconciliation, they decided to divorce. Larry was relocating to Charleston, three hours away from Charlotte.

"Bye, Dad," Kristy called from the front porch. As Larry plunked an almost four-year-old Gus onto the passenger seat of his white BMW, he swallowed hard and commanded himself not to lose it in front of the girls.

"Call us as soon as you get there," Heather said, running over to give him one last hug.

The move to Charleston had sounded good on paper. It meant a fresh start, both in real estate and in life. But now, saying good-bye to his girls, the moment felt anything but good. His throat tightened, and his eyes burned.

"I will. I promise." He pulled them both in tight. "I love you both very much—very, very much."

God, watch over them and protect them, he prayed as he backed out of his driveway—*out of Chris's driveway*, he corrected himself. He had signed over the house and everything in it to her, which made for light packing, but it also meant he really *was* starting over. All he had were some clothes, a trunk full of personal items, and Gus.

The pain of all he had lost haunted Larry during the trip. But as they turned off I-26 onto Meeting Street, Larry couldn't help but laugh at Gus. He was the picture of joy and happiness with his ears flopping wildly in the wind, his tongue hanging out of his mouth, and a stream of drool splattering the window.

A few blocks later, Larry turned into the parking lot of a nondescript apartment complex, pulled into a parking spot, and turned off the ignition. He got out, walked to the passenger door, and lifted Gus out of the car. "Looks like it's just you and me now, boy. What do you think? Are we ready for this?"

Gus let out a deep, throaty bark.

"Me too," Larry said, patting Gus's back. "Let's go see our new home."

As the months passed, Larry and Gus resumed their twice-daily walks, often ending up at the beach. Most days Larry enjoyed watching families interacting and letting children pet Gus. But on this particular day, Larry craved solitude, so he and Gus walked to the end of a small fishing pier. Larry sat on the wooden dock, and Gus plopped down beside him, then army-crawled his way to the edge of the pier to watch the lapping waves.

Larry's mind wandered. *How did I get here? How will I ever get back to where I was?* His heart sank with the pebble he tossed into the choppy waves. *Will I ever get back to where I was?*

His daughters were now in college, living their own lives. He and Chris rarely spoke, and when they did, it was usually strained. And building new real estate connections had proven to be a painfully slow and disappointing process.

He threw another pebble into the water.

You let this happen, he scolded himself. His shoulders sagged under the weight of the mental assault. *You had it all, and you lost it. You lost everything. You are a loser.*

A silent wail contorted his face and tightened every muscle.

He looked down at the water.

Darkness pressed in, taunting him. Ridiculing him. Daring him. He peered into the water. *I wonder how deep it is?* His breath quickened and his heart pounded in his ears. Then something touched his thigh, and Larry flinched. Gus was resting his paw on Larry's leg. The hound's deep-set eyes focused intently on Larry's, and he released a soft, mournful whimper.

Good old devoted, dependable Gus. His faithful friend who had been there through it all—every argument, every lost account, every sleepless night.

Larry scooted back from the edge, and Gus climbed into his lap.

"You've always been by my side." Though his mouth spoke the words to Gus, his heart spoke them to God. "I know I'm not alone. I just want what you want for me."

His silent tears of surrender dripped onto Gus's fur, and the two exhaled deeply together.

Therapy dogs. As Larry poured a second cup of early morning coffee, a realization began to take shape: *Gus acted like a therapy dog to me that night on the dock. Maybe God's nudge about therapy dogs wasn't out of left field after all.*

He had never thought of Gus as anything other than his long-eared sidekick, but the truth was, Gus had helped Larry in so many ways—staying close, keeping him busy and distracted, getting him outside, helping him meet people, and continually pointing his heart toward God.

And while that pivotal evening on the dock had changed nothing on the outside, it had changed everything on the inside. That evening, with Gus on his lap, Larry had surrendered his failures, his shattered dreams, his hope of future success, and his life plan to God.

Now, as he resumed his place in the recliner, more memories reeled through his mind.

As the year wore on, Larry started spending more time walking Gus along the waterfront, eating with him at outdoor cafes, and engaging in small talk with women who would stop the pair and want to pet Gus's ears.

"Who knew you were such a chick magnet?" Larry teased Gus one night after getting two phone numbers and making plans to meet a woman named Tina for dinner the next night.

But even as a chick magnet, Gus was not without his quirks—mainly his unique odor, an issue Larry was determined to address before his date.

"I'm not trying to hurt you," he said, struggling to hold on to the squirming, slippery hound in the bathtub. "I'm just trying to make you smell better. Between those ears constantly dragging on the ground and that waterproof coat of yours, you're not only a chick magnet, you're a dirt magnet!"

Gus pointed his nose to the ceiling and began to howl his displeasure. It was the same howl he'd used when Larry had wrestled him from under the bed and carried him to the bathroom—kind of like a cow impersonating an ambulance siren.

"Stay still, buddy. I just need to . . ."

Gus stopped howling long enough to give a vigorous shake, thoroughly soaking Larry.

After rinsing the soap out of Gus's coat, Larry lifted him from the tub and wrapped him in a fluffy white towel. The hound's howls of angst quickly turned to happy whimpers of delight.

"To know you is to love you," Larry mused.

Unfortunately, Larry's date did not agree. After enjoying a nice meal together, Larry had invited Tina over for a cup of coffee and to meet Gus. But no sooner did they walk into Larry's apartment when . . .

"Oh my," Tina exclaimed, holding her hand to her nose. "What is that smell?"

As if on cue, Gus sauntered around the corner.

"Is that *him*?" Tina pointed to Gus. "I didn't think such a cute dog could smell so . . . I mean, he has an unusual odor, doesn't he?"

Larry was more than familiar with the unique smell common to the breed, but he didn't necessarily consider it *bad*. And he certainly would never look at Gus the way Tina was looking at him now.

"Tina, I had a really nice time with you at dinner," he began, "but I can tell you don't care for Gus, and the thing is . . . we're a package deal. So maybe we should just call it a night."

Tina looked stunned, but Larry meant it. He had no interest in wasting time with someone who didn't love Gus—distinct smell and all.

Tina rolled her eyes and left.

"Well, boy, maybe I'm not as ready to enter the dating pool as I thought I was," Larry said as Gus's stubby little legs ran double-time to his best friend's side. "I guess it's just you and me again."

Larry and Gus resumed their comfortable routine of going on waterfront walks, watching ESPN together, and every few weeks, when he got a little too pungent, wrestling Gus into the bathtub.

🐾

A few years passed and Larry was offered a position in the real estate firm's Tampa office. After weighing the pros and cons—a fresh start versus moving farther away from his daughters—Larry decided on the fresh start.

"It's time for another road trip, Gus. You up for another adventure?"

Of course he was!

As it turned out, a fresh start had been just what Larry needed. He found a church where he felt welcome and encouraged, and a great town house close to the sparkling waters of Tampa Bay.

Larry and Gus continued their daily walks, though Gus, now ten, occasionally needed a little more encouragement to finish the route.

"Come on, you can do it," Larry encouraged, gently tugging on Gus's leash as he lay down on the grass. "I know your legs are tired, but we still have to walk back home."

Gus turned a disinterested eye toward Larry, then laid his head between his front legs. Larry had experienced this mid-walk revolt enough times to know it was pointless to fight it. So he just sat down in the grass next to him.

"It's okay," Larry said, rubbing Gus's ears. "I'll just sit here with you till you're ready to get up."

One day, as Larry waited for Gus to rally, he noticed people setting up a tent nearby and others with dogs congregating around it. "Let's check out what's happening over there," Larry said. Gus rose with a yawn and a shake of his ears, then slowly plodded toward the crowd. While Gus greeted the dogs and nearby humans, Larry approached a woman wearing a purple "Project PUP" shirt and handing out pamphlets.

"What does PUP stand for?" Larry asked.

She explained that Project PUP (Pets Uplifting People) was an organization that sent well-behaved dogs into nursing homes to visit residents.

"This little guy would be a perfect Project PUP dog!" The woman smiled, kneeling down to pet Gus. Before they left, she gave Larry the application forms to fill out.

That afternoon, Larry made an appointment for Gus to be evaluated by an American Kennel Club (AKC) certified dog trainer, and two weeks later, Gus had his Canine Good Citizen certification, a purple Project PUP bandanna, and the green light to represent Project PUP at a nursing home on Bayshore Boulevard.

Dressed in his Project PUP shirt, Larry stepped through the front door of the nursing home, equally nervous and excited. He checked in at the front desk and was escorted to a large room where residents sat in wheelchairs and at tables watching TV and playing games.

"Hi, doggie!" an elderly female voice called out.

Gus walked in her direction, stopping every four to five feet to allow people to stroke his back, eating up the attention as if it were a box of Milk-Bones that had tipped over and spilled its contents. He eagerly walked toward outstretched hands, soulfully gazed at lonely-looking residents, and happily sat beside those who wanted to talk to him.

One woman, sitting in a wheelchair off by herself, waved Gus over. "I had a little dog that looked just like you," she said, her voice weak and raspy. "He brought me such joy." As Gus wagged his tail happily, the woman's face transformed from distant and vacant to joy-filled. "My dog's name was Maggie, and she sure would have liked you."

Larry spent several minutes visiting with the woman. She thanked him for bringing Gus to meet her and asked if he would bring him back soon.

"I sure will."

"You were amazing in there, buddy!" Larry beamed on the way home. He couldn't contain his joy. His career was taking off again. He was making friends. He was attending church. And he and Gus were going to start spending their free time bringing happiness to lonely people. Everything was good.

And then . . .

"What's the matter, bud? Don't you want your dinner?"

Gus responded by raising his right eyebrow slightly. Larry sat on the sofa next to Gus and studied his dear friend. Gus's eyes had been looking different recently. More tired. Droopier. Larry laid his hand on Gus's belly, and a low rumble vibrated from the dog's throat. Larry flinched. Gus *never* growled.

Larry made an appointment with the vet for the next day.

Once there, Larry explained that Gus hadn't been as interested in eating lately, but at ten years of age, he just assumed his dog's appetite was slowing down with the rest of him. The vet's brow furrowed as he palpated Gus's belly. Minutes later, Gus was getting X-rays done. When the vet came back into the room, the look on his face told Larry everything he needed to know.

"I'm afraid Gus's stomach has twisted on itself and is cutting off the blood supply to his digestive system," the vet explained. "We can try surgery, but at his age and with the severity of his case, he likely won't survive the procedure."

Larry felt the breath leave his chest. He lowered himself to his knees and rubbed Gus's ears. His dog—his best friend, confidant, and beloved sidekick—looked up at him with trusting eyes. The vet said he would give Larry a few minutes to make his decision and quietly exited the room.

"Oh Gus, what am I going to do without you?" Larry whispered, his tears being absorbed into Gus's fur.

Larry swallowed against the pain rising in his throat. He kissed the top of Gus's head, then the tip of each ear. He laid his head against Gus's back. Larry wanted to tell the vet to do whatever he had to do to save his friend. He would pay any price. Do anything. But he knew. As surely as he knew God had sent Gus to him, Larry knew it was time to let the faithful dog go.

After the vet gave Gus a strong painkiller, Larry cradled Gus in his arms.

"You are the world's best dog, and I am going to miss you so much."

The doctor gave Gus a second injection, and Larry held his friend until Gus's heart stopped beating. Larry forced himself to stand and then slowly walked out of the room. He had never felt more alone than he did leaving the vet's office without Gus. He stopped to collect himself in the parking lot and immediately thought of Gus's mid-walk naps. An involuntary chuckle quickly turned into a sob, and Larry's tears began to fall.

It took a long time for the weight of grief to lessen. Every reminder of Gus felt like a blow to his heart. Larry tried to stay busy. He took on more projects at work, flew out to visit his daughters, and started playing golf.

Over time, he started to smile and laugh again, but he didn't think he would ever feel truly whole or wholly loved again . . . until he met Susan.

Larry set his coffee cup down on the counter and shook off the painful memories of those last minutes with Gus—memories he hadn't let himself think about for almost ten years. And yet, the significance of Gus's life and how he acted like Larry's personal therapy dog wasn't lost on him.

"Therapy dogs," he repeated again. The words hadn't come out of nowhere. Could God be speaking to him?

But what would he say to Susan? They had only been married for five years, and he had already taken her to hurricane-ravaged Louisiana to help feed victims of Katrina, to Tanzania to build churches, and to south Florida to build houses with Habitat for Humanity. Could he really ask her to join him on another wild adventure? And why would God ask him to do something with therapy dogs now?

Maybe I heard him wrong, he rationalized. *Maybe my subconscious had just been remembering Gus, or maybe I dreamed about him last night and he was just on my mind this morning.*

Larry's pulse began racing as his heart accepted what his mind was still fighting.

Trust me, not your own understanding.

"Okay, Lord, I will do whatever you want me to do," Larry spoke aloud. "But, um . . . I think you might have to bring me a dog first."

CHAPTER TWO

LARRY HARDLY NOTICED the passing scenery as he drove to his office. His thoughts were consumed with therapy dogs, though he still couldn't understand why. Neither could Susan when he had filled her in on the unusual turn his morning had taken. She had been pouring her coffee when Larry walked into the kitchen and blurted out, "I think God wants me to do something with therapy dogs."

She stared blankly at him for several moments before taking a sip from her mug, then asked him to repeat what he had just said.

"I know it sounds strange, but I heard his voice so clearly, Susie. My heart started shouting yes before I even had a chance to think about how crazy it all sounded."

"It does sound a bit . . . odd," Susan agreed. "But you seem very excited. And I know what happens when you get excited about an idea." She set her coffee mug on the counter. "Obviously, I have a lot of questions, but I know you love dogs—we both do. And I know how much you miss Gus. So if you really feel like God is calling you to do something with dogs, then we'll figure it out."

He kissed her forehead and hugged her tight. Her unwavering belief in him made him feel like the richest man in the world. "I love you so much."

She squeezed him back. "I love you too."

The blare of a horn brought Larry back to the present rush-hour traffic in Tampa. Twenty minutes later, he was in his office reviewing a four-million-dollar offer on a shopping center when his business partner, Brad, arrived.

"Well, good morning," Larry said, smiling.

The younger man waved Larry into his office. They went over the day's agenda and talked about the two presentations they had scheduled later that morning, then the conversation turned to their families. Larry always enjoyed hearing about Brad and his wife, Karen's, adventures with their five children. He deeply respected Brad for how he prioritized his family. When Brad asked about Susan, Larry joked about not knowing what color his bedroom would be when he returned. Still chuckling, Larry rose to leave, then paused in the doorway.

"Everything okay?" Brad asked.

Larry hesitated. Even though he was still mulling over the early-morning words he had heard from God, he was compelled to get his partner's opinion. But would Brad understand? *I don't even understand.*

Regardless, Larry realized he wanted—needed—to talk about this with someone. Especially someone with such strong faith and integrity.

Larry walked back into Brad's office and sat down again. He wanted to accurately describe what his mindset had been that morning and to paint a clear picture of the situation. Mostly, though, he wanted to convey the way his heart had been touched by what he felt so strongly was God's voice.

However, what came out of his mouth was, "I think God wants me to get a therapy dog."

Well, so much for context, Larry mused. When Brad's mouth opened and closed twice without any sound emerging, Larry filled in more of the details—the verses from Proverbs, asking God what he wanted Larry to do and hearing "therapy dogs," culminating in the unexpected memories of Gus.

"So I don't know. It just feels like maybe I'm supposed to do something with a therapy dog. But I have no idea *what* exactly."

Larry could usually read his partner so well that they could communicate across a table without uttering a word. But now Larry had no idea what Brad was thinking. *Does he think I've lost it?* he worried as Brad continued to sit in silent observation.

Larry could feel his cheeks flushing. As he was thinking of a way to politely exit his partner's office, Brad sat back with a wide smile.

"I don't think I've ever seen you this excited," he said. "Not even when we sold that industrial park last year. And while I don't have any answers for you, I definitely think you should keep an open mind, continue praying about it, and see where God leads."

Larry let out a breath he didn't know he had been holding, stood, and shook his partner's hand.

"So you don't think I'm crazy?" Larry said, laughing with relief.

"Well, not about this at least," his business partner joked.

After thanking Brad for his time, Larry walked back into his office to prepare for their ten o'clock meeting. *No more dog talk,* Larry said to himself. *It's time to get to work.*

Larry stayed busy with paperwork, meetings, and phone calls for the rest of his workday, yet the image of a dog lying quietly at his feet kept diverting his attention. His mind was like a multiplex movie theater with images, ideas, and thoughts filling every screen. One screen was the biggest, loudest, and most central, but the others were always running—even if they were a little out of focus at times. As Larry went about his tasks, one of the smaller screens kept playing a continuous loop of happy dogs interacting with people.

Later that evening, after dinner, he and Susan relaxed on the sofa. It was their habit to sit together and review the day's events, something Larry loved doing with his wife. "I haven't been able to stop thinking about therapy dogs," he told her. "In fact, when a new client mentioned getting a puppy, I almost asked if he was going to train the puppy to become a therapy dog."

Susan chuckled and rubbed Larry's shoulder.

He continued, "But enough about all that. Tell me about your day."

She recounted what they had discussed at Bible Study Fellowship, then she paused and smiled. "And today I met Sister Agnes, a new customer for Meals on Wheels."

Her smile was so big, tiny creases were forming at the corners of her eyes. "Oh, she is the sweetest woman, Larry. She taught at a Catholic school in Miami before retiring here. She lives in the Tall Pines retirement community, and from the way she was talking, I get the feeling she's the self-appointed welcome committee and caregiver of the place."

Then she looked past Larry and sighed deeply. "I don't know why, but I felt such a strong connection to her. She doesn't have any family nearby. In fact, I got the impression she doesn't have any family anywhere. I just wish there was something I could do to bless her like she's blessed so many others."

Suddenly, the movie screen playing images of happy dogs moved front and center in Larry's mind. He sat up straight.

"Susie, what if we took a dog to visit Sister Agnes—you know, like a *therapy* dog?"

Susan tilted her head the way she did when she was stuck on a crossword puzzle. She was quiet for a moment. Then . . .

"I think it's a brilliant idea! But there's one problem. We don't have a dog, remember?"

"Oh, right," Larry acknowledged sheepishly. "Well, if God can put an idea in my head and a nun in your path, I'm sure he can bring us a dog, right?"

Suddenly, Susan sprang to her feet so quickly she startled Larry. "I think I know where we can get a dog!"

🐾

"I still can't believe we didn't think of Cody right away," Susan beamed at Larry as she rang the doorbell. "He'd be perfect!"

A moment later, Susan's daughter, Brooke, opened the door and her six-year-old Golden Retriever, Cody, came bounding out. The reddish-brown dog ran straight to Larry, wagging his tail and greeting him with I'm-so-happy-to-see-you sounds.

"Well, hello there, Cody." Larry knelt down just in time for Cody's tongue to land on his cheek.

"Hi, Mom, Larry," Brooke said, embracing each one. "Come on in."

As they followed Brooke into the house and made themselves comfortable, Larry got right to the point. "We wanted to talk to you about an idea I had—or rather an idea I think God gave me."

"Yes, you mentioned on the phone yesterday something about borrowing Cody?" Brooke began.

Larry chuckled. "Yeah, I guess we were a little vague." He leaned forward and Susan laid her hand on his back. "I feel like God wants us to show his love to others by bringing a dog—well, by bringing Cody, that is—to visit them."

At the sound of his name, Cody walked and placed his head on Larry's knee. Larry stroked the tuft of fur on the top of Cody's head as he continued. "I know firsthand how much a dog can help you not feel alone. And I think God is calling me—" he glanced back at Susan—"calling *us* to do something with therapy dogs. Maybe just one visit, maybe more. I don't really know. I just know that I feel God leading me to help people experience his love through dogs. But since we don't have a dog, we thought maybe you might let us borrow Cody?"

He sat back and took a deep breath. Sitting across from Brooke, trying to explain his personal, private moment with the Lord, made him suddenly feel vulnerable and unsure. *Am I putting Brooke in an awkward position? Will she feel obligated or pressured to say yes? Will I feel rejected and silly if she says no?* Susan squeezed Larry's hand and gave him a reassuring smile.

"I think it's a great idea," Brooke said, breaking the silence.

"Really?" Larry and Susan asked in unison.

"Really!" Brooke laughed. "Bryan and I talked about it last night. With him out visiting job sites and me at the VA most days, Cody is left alone a lot. This would give Cody something to do, and we both like the idea of him being active—especially if it means helping people. And since he's already been through obedience training and has his Canine Good Citizen certificate, you can get started right away."

Susan had tried to assure Larry that Brooke, a licensed counselor, would understand the value of therapy dogs, but Larry had been too nervous to make any assumptions.

"Thank you so much," Larry gushed. "I . . . *we* really appreciate it. Cody is so well-behaved that I'm sure he'll make a wonderful impression on Sister Agnes."

Brooke raised a questioning eyebrow.

"She's a sweet elderly woman I met," Susan explained. "And I really think she's going to love Cody."

"How could she not?" Larry said. "What do you think, Cody? Are you ready to start working as a therapy dog?" Cody immediately rolled onto his back.

"I think we can take that as a yes," Brooke said, laughing.

"We'll pick him up next Tuesday," Larry explained. "And just to be clear . . . I am just borrowing him. I understand Cody is *your* dog. I promise to always bring him back here."

After saying good night to Brooke and Cody, Larry realized on the drive home that everything was starting to make sense. He and Susan would take Cody to meet Sister Agnes and hopefully bring some joy to her life. Susan would feel empowered to help Sister Agnes. And Larry would be able to support his wife and make a difference to a lonely woman. Yes, it all made perfect sense now. And it felt entirely doable. A small weekend ministry sounded like the perfect way for Larry and Susan to quietly ease into their retirement years.

CHAPTER THREE

LARRY STOOD OUTSIDE of Sister Agnes's small prefabricated home, holding the end of Cody's leash in his hand and uncertainty in his heart. *How will she react to Cody? How will Cody react to her?* What had seemed like an inspired idea two weeks earlier suddenly felt foolish and rash.

"She's going to love Cody," Susan whispered, sensing Larry's hesitation.

He took a deep breath and looked at Cody. While Cody wasn't an official therapy dog yet, Larry hoped the dog would quickly step into the role—and title. The retriever certainly looked the part in his black vest with the words "Therapy Dog" in red lettering.

Larry had started preparing, too, by reading articles and books about working with therapy dogs and about therapy dog ministries. That is how he had learned about the importance of having a therapy dog wear a special vest or harness to let them know when they were "going to work." Larry had no doubt that Cody got the message as he sat in the back of the SUV with rapt attention. Cody was clearly ready. Larry was not. But when Cody let out an excited—and impatient—bark, Larry realized that ready or not, it was time to make their first official visit.

As they approached Sister Agnes's front door, Larry took Susan's hand and whispered a prayer. "God, give us the words to say. Let us be your hands and feet—and wagging tail," he added, patting Cody's head.

He straightened his shoulders and knocked on the door. When Sister Agnes opened it, Larry surprised himself with his confident greeting.

"Well, hello there," he said, reaching out his hand. "I'm Larry Randolph." Cody tugged at the leash in Larry's other hand. "I sure hope you like dogs," he laughed, struggling to keep Cody from jumping up, "because this one sure is excited to meet you."

A petite woman with short, white curly hair and a wide smile nodded and said she had been expecting them. "This is Cody," Larry continued, "and you already know my wife, Susan. Is it okay if we come in and visit for a while?"

Sister Agnes's wide smile remained on her face as she invited them in, but she nervously glanced at Cody when the eighty-five-pound dog bounded into the tiny six-hundred-square-foot home, literally pulling Larry into the house behind him.

Maybe Cody and I should have gone through some kind of formal training program.

The six-year-old Golden had been through basic obedience classes as a puppy and was the most gentle and well-behaved dog Larry had ever known. He knew his furry friend would settle down quickly, but by the way Agnes was sitting on the edge of her recliner with her eyes following the retriever's every move, Larry feared his strategy of letting Cody just be Cody might not have been the best idea.

Susan took a seat at the small kitchen table directly across from Sister Agnes and began commiserating with her about the stifling hot weather. With Agnes temporarily occupied, Larry allowed Cody a few minutes to explore his new environment. He held loosely to Cody's leash as the dog walked from the living room to the adjoining kitchen—stopping every few feet to smell the baseboards and carpet. He poked his nose into Agnes's small bedroom, raised his head toward the ceiling, and sniffed the air, fragrant with essences of Listerine, Bengay, and laundry soap.

"Okay, Cody, let's go sit with Sister Agnes now," Larry said, giving a gentle tug to get the dog's attention.

Without hesitating, Cody made a beeline to their new friend. He laid his head on her lap and let out a loud sigh.

"I make the same sound when I sit down," she laughed, patting Cody's head.

Realizing he had found a willing hand to pet him, Cody turned and sat beside her—keeping his head near her hand. She smiled and happily obliged.

"You never get any attention, do you?" Sister Agnes teased, visibly relaxing and warming up to the dog.

"Oh, he's never short on hands to pet him," Larry assured her. "But he sure does like you. Look at the big smile he has and how his tail is wagging."

"I'm happy to meet him too."

Larry asked Sister Agnes how she was feeling.

"Oh, I can't complain," she replied, her easy smile bearing

witness to the truth of her words. "I have a comfortable home, a nice little community, new friends, and the love of a good God. What else could I need?"

During their almost-hour-long visit, Sister Agnes described growing up on a farm in Minnesota where she developed a deep appreciation for animals and nature. Larry gathered that while Agnes was not a huge animal lover, she respected them and felt kindly toward them. After answering several questions about her childhood, Agnes steered the conversation toward her time as a teacher.

"I loved every one of my students—even the ones who tested my patience and my commitment to the faith," she added with a wink.

Larry could easily picture her leading a classroom and had no doubt she had been a strict but fair teacher.

Sister Agnes got up and walked to her small refrigerator where she pulled out slices of key lime pie and set them in front of Larry and Susan, along with tall glasses of water. As they began to eat, the nun settled back in her recliner with Cody resuming his position beside her.

"Most people here don't have any family so we become each other's family," she said, absentmindedly stroking Cody's ears. "I guess you could say this place has become my new ministry. I check in on those who can't get out anymore. I pray with those who are sick and sit with those who are lonely. I can't give them much, but I can give them my presence."

That's what I want our therapy dog visits to be—a ministry of presence, Larry thought. Of being present with Sister Agnes. And maybe even a few others at some point down the road. Nothing big or earth-shattering, but something—a small act of kindness and companionship in their day.

When it was time to leave, Larry and Susan thanked Sister Agnes for her hospitality and hugged her on their way out. The nun held on to her walker with one hand and patted Cody's head with the other all the way to the door.

"Come back and visit me again soon," she called out after them.

And they did—the very next week.

Sister Agnes met them at the door with a warm smile and Nutter Butter cookies on the table. Cody eyed the cookies, but he didn't whine or beg. Larry didn't want Cody to eat treats during a visit because he might become more focused on food than on making new friends. When the visit was over and they were back at the car, Larry would reward Cody with treats.

Twenty minutes into their visit, Sister Agnes surprised Larry and Susan with a request.

"My neighbor, Shirley, who lives two doors down, has been terribly lonesome since her husband died two months ago. Would you mind taking Cody by for a quick visit before you leave?" Larry noticed her eyes held a mischievous twinkle. "I called her a little while ago and said you would be stopping by."

Larry laughed. "Sister Agnes, I'm beginning to understand that you are a woman who knows how to get things done."

After finishing their visit with her, they walked to Shirley's house.

"Yes?" a raspy voice called after Larry knocked on the door.

"Hello, Shirley," Larry called back. "We are Larry and Susan Randolph. Agnes sent us over to visit you. May we come in for a few minutes?"

"Oh, you're the dog people!" Shirley all but shouted, opening the door. "Come in. Come in!"

Cody bounded forward and placed his head under Shirley's hand. "Well, aren't you a handsome fella. Come in and sit a spell."

Shirley shuffled into her living room and motioned for Larry and Susan to sit on the small sofa. Larry kept Cody close to his side as they sat, wanting to dissuade him from exploring Shirley's house as he had done her neighbor's.

"Now, you let that dog be," Shirley reprimanded. "He came all this way to visit me, so you let him come see me."

Shirley's jovial expression belied her demanding tone. *All bark and no bite,* Larry mused.

Shirley clapped her hands, and Cody quickly complied—but only after looking back at Larry for approval. *Good boy,* Larry silently praised.

"Well, aren't you just the sweetest thing," Shirley cooed, leaning her head toward Cody's.

The woman's thick shoulder-length gray hair brushed against Cody as she nuzzled him. Larry noticed a large framed photo of a younger Shirley all dressed up, standing beside a dapper man in a suit. The love between them was undeniable.

"That's my Joe," she said.

"Sister Agnes said you lost him recently," Susan spoke softly. "We are so sorry for your loss, Shirley."

Shirley nodded gratefully as her eyes grew misty. "Sixty-three years, and it wasn't enough. He was sitting right here when his heart just gave out," she said, patting her chair. "I told him his heart was too big. That man was always going out of his way to help folks. Helping 'em move, listening to their woes, giving people money we didn't have. Didn't matter what they needed, my Joe wanted to help."

"Joe sounds like he was a wonderful man," Larry offered.

"I miss him so very much."

She sat back in her chair but kept a hand on Cody. "We had a dog named Ginger, an Irish Setter that Joe got from a coworker. She was sweeter than apple pie smothered in vanilla ice cream. Had her while we were raising babies. Good dog. Great with kids too." Shirley's voice trailed off as she stroked Cody. "I forgot how much I love dogs. My Joe sure would have loved you, too, Mr. Cody."

After making plans to visit again soon, they exchanged hugs and Shirley gave Cody one last pat.

It was a quiet ride home. The visit with Shirley had gone so well that Larry started wondering if they should visit more residents in the Tall Pines retirement community. Not someday in the future. Now. He noticed Susan seemed lost in her own thoughts.

"What are you thinking about?" he asked.

"That I absolutely loved visiting Agnes and Shirley. I know we talked about keeping this ministry very small, but I really think we should visit more people."

He reached over and grabbed her hand. "Then we are both thinking the same thing."

Twenty minutes later, they pulled into Brooke and Bryan's driveway to drop Cody off.

"Cody, once again, you were a natural," Larry praised, opening the rear door of his SUV.

Cody bounded out of the car, ran in two tight circles, relieved himself in the grass, and ran right back to Larry's side, ready for their next adventure.

"We'll do it again soon, I promise," Larry said, kneeling to plant a kiss on Cody's long snout.

33

Brooke and Bryan were still at work, so Larry and Susan let Cody in, gave him a treat, and topped off his water bowl before leaving.

The couple spent the next few days praying for clarity and asking God to show them the next steps to take if he did in fact want them to do more with Cody. Larry continued reading through Proverbs every morning, and he also began writing his prayers and ideas in a journal.

One morning as he was asking God to make his plan and will clear, the memory of sitting with Gus outside of the Project PUP tent popped into his mind. He smiled as he remembered all the dogs sniffing each other and playing together while their humans received information about the program. *They were able to take dogs into a lot of different nursing homes because they had so many different dogs.* The realization—which seemed more like a revelation—made Larry feverishly write down a prayer as the hot August sun began to rise.

> *God, I sense that you are calling me to share your love with the sick, the lonely, the elderly, children, and all who need hope, and to do so through dogs. Dogs that you have created to be a vessel for your compassion and kindness.*

With the Project PUP tent image fresh in his mind, Larry began to jot down some ideas:

1. *Invite others to join us.*
2. *Train and equip volunteers to make impactful (and safe) visits.*

3. Observe dogs and ensure they are well-behaved and up-to-date on shots.

He remembered the purple shirts the Project PUP volunteers were wearing to make it easy to identify that they were affiliated with the program—and how much Gus liked wearing his purple Project PUP bandanna.

4. Design shirts for volunteers and vests or bandannas for dogs.
5. Come up with a list of places to make visits.
6. Set up a rotation for visits.

Larry tapped his pen against his forehead. He was sure there was more to write down, but this felt like enough—more than enough for now. But something was still missing. Larry got up from the recliner and walked to the patio door. He loved the early dawn view of the golf course in the distance, especially when it was trimmed with a thin ribbon of fog like this morning.

"Lord, I want this ministry to be what you want it to be," he prayed aloud, surprised by how comfortable he was with the thought of his on-the-side therapy dog visits becoming a full-fledged ministry. "But I still feel like there's something I need to do. Something you would have me do before we go any further. Will you show me what that is?"

When no message rang down from the heavens, Larry went to shower and get ready for the day. When he reentered the living room, Susan was working on her Bible study homework.

"Larry, I've been thinking about where we should look for volunteers," she said, setting her workbook aside. "Talk to Pastor

Matthew. Maybe the church will partner with us. I'm sure there are people there with dogs who would love to do something like this. And besides, if nothing else, they could pray for us as we try to figure this out, right?"

The words were from Susan's lips, but Larry had no doubt they were from God's heart.

"That's a great idea. I'll call the church today."

🐾

A week later, Larry and Cody followed a friendly woman named Donna into a small conference room off the senior pastor's office in Van Dyke Church. She invited Larry to take a seat and then knelt in front of Cody.

"You are just the cutest dog in the whole wide world, aren't you? I think you need to come visit me every single day."

Cody responded to Donna's praise with a wet kiss on her cheek. She laughed and told Larry that the pastor would be in shortly.

"You ready, boy?" Larry asked as the dog leaned against his leg.

Larry had no doubt Cody was ready, but he was suddenly more nervous than he ever had been. *What if Pastor Matthew doesn't think the church should be involved in a therapy dog ministry? What if he doesn't like dogs?* Larry sat up straight with the last thought. *I should have asked if it was okay to bring Cody!*

Larry ran his damp palms against his pant legs.

"Be a good boy, Cody," he pleaded as Matthew Hartsfield's office door opened.

Larry rose to shake the pastor's hand. "It's good to see you, Pastor. I hope you don't mind that I brought Cody with me."

"I'm very glad you did. I'm looking forward to learning more about this new ministry of yours."

Matthew motioned for Larry to retake his seat, while he sat on the opposite sofa. Then, as if Cody had been given some secret signal, he bounded up so suddenly Larry didn't have time to grab hold of his leash. Cody leaped onto the sofa, and—to Larry's horror—plopped right on Pastor Matthew's lap.

"Oooofff," Matthew exclaimed as all eighty-five pounds of Cody landed on him.

Larry was mortified. "Cody, come!" He had never seen Cody jump on someone like that before. *So much for any church support*, he thought woefully.

If Cody heard Larry's command, he chose to ignore it. Instead, he swiped his tongue across the pastor's cheek and snuggled in closer. Larry wanted to bolt from the room, but instead he lunged toward Cody. He expected to see an annoyed expression on Matthew's face—it was the least he deserved. Especially considering the man's black pants were now covered in dog hair.

"I am so sorry," Larry began, reaching for Cody's collar.

But instead of an irritated expression, the pastor was beaming, and his shoulders were shaking with laughter as he nuzzled Cody's face.

"You sure know how to make someone feel loved, don't you, boy?" he chuckled.

"Cody, down. Come," Larry commanded, a little more gently this time. Cody complied, and Larry led the dog back to the other sofa, keeping a tight grip on his collar. "Sit, Cody. *Stay*." He emphasized the last word and held tightly to Cody's leash.

"I am so sorry about that," Larry repeated, his cheeks hot with embarrassment. "He has never done that before, and I will make *sure* he never does it again. He's been so well-behaved on our previous visits. I don't know what got into him."

Matthew brushed the hair from his pants and waved off Larry's apology. "Oh, I think he just knew that I needed a good laugh today. I've met with several people who are hurting and angry and it's—" he cleared his throat and gave a slight shake of his head—"well, let's just say it's been a hard day. But Cody here, well, he knew just what I needed, didn't you?"

Cody's tail swooshed against the carpet, his ears raised and mouth open in expectation.

"May I?" Matthew asked, extending his hand toward the dog.

"Cody, easy," Larry said, rising from his seat.

He walked the dog back to the pastor and told him to sit. Cody rested his head contentedly on Matthew's knee.

"So, tell me more about this ministry. What are you hoping to see come from this? What do you feel God is calling you to do?"

Larry took a deep breath. "Well," he began, "the short version is that I want to minister to people—to bring them hope and God's love—through therapy dogs. I believe people can encounter God's love and compassion through dogs—sometimes even more so than they can through people.

"I experienced the unconditional love of a dog named Gus at a very difficult time in my own life. He constantly pointed my heart back to God. I think it was the way he was always there for me, always happy to see me, always looking at me with soulful eyes that seemed to see the best in me—it made me want to live up to his view of me."

Larry licked his suddenly dry lips. "As you know, probably more than most, people in this world are hurting—some are hurting really bad. But most of them won't step foot in a church. And many of them physically can't. But the church can go to them. And maybe in this case, the church—or at least God's presence and love—could go to them wrapped in dog fur with a wagging, happy tail."

Larry leaned back against the cushion, suddenly feeling more confident than ever that he was meant to start and run this ministry.

Ministry.

Not a part-time service project with Susan. Not a weekend volunteer effort. But a ministry.

"How do you see this working?" Matthew asked. "What do you see as far as structure and day-to-day operations?"

Twenty minutes earlier, Larry would have struggled to answer that question. But now, he saw it clearly.

"I see teams—one or two people with a dog—all of them easily identified as being affiliated with the ministry by wearing the same shirts and dog vests. I don't want to hide that we are there to bring God's love; I want people to know we are a faith-based ministry. To that end, I want cards to leave with the people after we visit, with a prayer on one side and our contact information on the other. And I would like to partner with the church somehow, possibly even making this a *church* ministry."

Larry risked a quick glance at the pastor to see how that last sentence was received. But Matthew wasn't looking at him. His attention seemed to be on Cody.

Larry continued, "I do have a full-time job, so I could probably use some help keeping track of volunteers, visits, and canine certifications. In all my reading and studying about therapy dogs, I've learned that the best practice is to have the dogs certified through the Canine Good Citizen test to ensure that they have mastered basic manners and are well-behaved. So we will need to keep track of that. We will also offer general training for volunteers, but once like-minded volunteers have gone through a brief orientation and the dogs have received their certification, the teams could start making visits and, Lord willing, bring love and joy to those they encounter."

Just then, Donna came into the room with two bottles of water for the men and a Styrofoam cup of water for Cody that Donna held for him as he drank. Larry closed his eyes and took a sip from his bottle. For the first time, he could *see* the ministry. He could *see* people encountering God's love, light shining into dark places, smiles on weary faces, and hurting people discovering hope. He could *see* wagging tails and wet noses being the vessels of God's love. He hoped Matthew could see the same vision, but even if he didn't, Larry knew he was meant to do this.

"Let's do it!"

"Really?" Larry blinked in surprise.

"Yes, I can see the vision you're casting. And I think this ministry has the potential to impact many people with the power of the gospel. And as long as *you* run the ministry—all of the day-to-day operations, the design, planning, and training—our church will support you in prayer and with volunteers. I could even lend you one of our wonderful administrative assistants whenever you need an extra set of hands."

Larry could barely take it all in. But Matthew's expression suddenly changed. He looked apologetic.

"Unfortunately, we aren't able to offer you financial support at this time. I'm hopeful that could be something we could do in the future, but our budget simply won't support that right now."

Since the church's financial support wasn't something that even had crossed Larry's mind to ask for, he wasn't disappointed—although he did make a mental note to talk to Susan about financial needs of a ministry that had just grown in vision and scope in the last twenty minutes.

"If you're open to it, I'd love to have you come speak to the congregation and tell them about the ministry."

"I would be honored!"

Before Larry and Cody left, Matthew prayed for them— thanking God for the gift of dogs, asking for his favor over the initiative, for wisdom and discernment for Larry, and for God to bring the right people at the right time to join them. Matthew knelt down to pet Cody, and the intuitive retriever leaned his head against the pastor's neck and exhaled.

"Thank you for being Jesus in fur to me today."

Larry found it hard to contain the emotion rising in his throat as he and Cody left the room.

There was much to do, much to discuss, and much to decide. But as Larry drove Cody back to his house to tell Susan the good news, all he could think about was the phrase Pastor Matthew had used: *Jesus in fur.*

Larry didn't know exactly what the phrase meant, how theologically accurate it might be, or how to teach a dog to do that, but he did know that was what he wanted Cody and any other dogs that joined the ministry to be for people: Jesus wrapped in fur.

CHAPTER FOUR

"WELL, SISTER AGNES," Larry said, six days after his meeting with Pastor Matthew, "it looks like we're going to make this an official therapy dog ministry."

Cody was standing in front of Sister Agnes, getting his velvety ears rubbed, while Susan quietly unloaded the groceries they had brought her. During their previous visit, Susan had noticed how bare the pantry was, and she had suggested to Larry that they pick up a few things for her. Agnes had protested the offering when they arrived, saying they shouldn't spend their hard-earned money on her. But when they insisted, she graciously thanked them.

"The church we attend is going to endorse the ministry and help us recruit volunteers, and one of the administrative assistants is going to help us keep track of everything. We are so excited to see what God is going to do through this ministry. And we owe a great deal to you."

"Oh pish, I didn't do a thing other than open my door. But I'm so happy. It's wonderful news! I could tell the first time you came here that you were made to do this work. When people are doing God's work, they have a light about them—a joy that comes from doing what you were put on this earth to do."

Larry had never thought about this newly formed ministry as being his calling. But then again, it hadn't even been on his radar until two months ago. There was no denying the joy and fulfillment he felt when he made visits with Cody, but was it *God's work*? Was it really what he was put on this earth to do? Now—at the age of sixty? He didn't know. He was just glad to be doing it.

"Thank you for saying that, Agnes."

"I speak the truth—and only the truth. Don't you forget that."

"Yes, ma'am."

"So what are you going to call it?"

Larry and Susan looked at each other. They hadn't talked about a name. In fact, they hadn't even *thought* about it until now.

"Well," Larry began, "I guess we're going to call it the Therapy Dog Ministry."

Agnes looked from Larry to Susan back to Larry with a barely restrained smile on her friendly face. "It's certainly not the most original name I've ever heard. But at least folks will know what you're doing."

They spent the rest of the visit with Cody lying at Agnes's feet. She was excited about planning a dinner for her neighbors with some of the food Larry and Susan had given her.

"You know," Agnes said, rising from her chair, "I think I'll go invite one of them now. Why don't you come with me, and I'll introduce you to Sam. He's a bit rough around the edges." She lowered her voice as if the topic of their discussion was in the next room instead of next door. "He's a recovering alcoholic and has been estranged from his family for years, but he's got a good heart under his curmudgeonly exterior."

Cody panted excitedly, but Larry was feeling a little less enthusiastic about stopping in on someone who hadn't asked them to come. Yet they followed Agnes, with Cody leading the way.

A short, stocky man with salt-and-pepper hair, a chin of white stubble, and two deep grooves between his bushy eyebrows opened the door.

"Who are they?" he asked Agnes gruffly. "And why do they have a dog?"

"Oh, you hush up now, Sam," Agnes soothed. "These nice people came to visit me, and now we are visiting you. And they brought their sweet dog along because people like dogs. Now, you be nice and let us in."

Sam grunted as he swung the door open. Cody sniffed the man's hand. Sam pulled it away. The small house smelled of cigarette smoke and burnt popcorn.

"Thank you for letting us visit," Larry said, wishing Sam had left the door open to allow some airflow. "Sister Agnes was telling us what a good neighbor you are."

Sam eyed him suspiciously. "Did she now? I find that hard to believe."

Agnes rose to her full height of five feet one inch and waved her index finger in Sam's weatherworn face. Cody lowered his head and leaned his weight against Larry. *Smart dog*, Larry thought.

"Now you listen here," Agnes began. "You *are* a good neighbor —albeit a crotchety one. And if you'd just button your lips and listen, these nice people brought me a lot of groceries—too much for one old woman to eat. So I'm going to fix a nice dinner tomorrow—for you, Shirley, Novie, and me. Now you invite us to sit down and visit or I'm taking back my invitation."

Larry didn't know if he should laugh, clap, or salute. He had never seen this spunky side of her. He had seen glimpses of Sister Agnes the schoolteacher, but this was more like Sister Agnes the drill sergeant.

Sam didn't say a word. He slunk over to a small black leather sofa and swept the magazines, mail, and socks that were covering it onto the floor. Then he moved a pile of rumpled clothes from a worn recliner to a small kitchen table and motioned for them to sit while he took one of the three mismatched chairs around the table and moved it to the main room.

Cody sat next to Larry and rested his head on the arm of the sofa, watching the man sitting across from him with his arms tightly folded. The older man mumbled something that sounded a lot like "meddling old woman," but Larry wasn't sure.

"We appreciate you letting us visit you," Larry tried again. "My wife, Susan, and I are starting a therapy dog ministry." Sam's eyebrows furrowed.

Larry cleared his throat and tried to clarify. "We want to bring God's love and joy to people through dogs like Cody."

The lines between Sam's eyebrows deepened.

"God's love?" He huffed. "Listen, you seem like nice enough people, and I imagine that dog of yours will make plenty of people happy and whatnot. But when it comes to God, you're wasting your time with me. He don't want nothin' to do with me. And let's just say the feeling's mutual. So you best be on your way and find some other people to visit."

Sam leaned back in his chair with a forceful sigh.

There was so much Larry wanted to say—he wanted to share

verses about God's love; to speak of times in his own life when he had felt forgotten by God. He wanted to share words others had spoken to him during times of doubt and despair, and yet he hesitated, unsure how his well-meaning words would be received. Instead, he offered a silent plea for divine help. As he did, Cody stood up and walked directly toward Sam. Sensing the dog's purpose and curious to see how it would be received, Larry allowed the leash to drag behind him.

The Golden sat down in front of Sam and rested his head on the man's leg. Sam's head jerked up. Larry feared he was going to yell at Cody, but instead, he simply stared at the dog. Sam slowly unfolded his arms and held his hands together. Cody nosed his head under Sam's right hand. Larry held his breath as the man's left hand moved toward Cody's head.

"What are you coming over here for?" Sam asked the dog. "You don't want to sit by a grumpy old coot."

Sam waved the dog away. But Cody didn't move. He kept his head on Sam's leg and his gaze fixed on his face. Susan grabbed Larry's knee.

"What do you want with me?" Sam asked, his hands moving to frame Cody's face. "I've got nothing for you."

"He just wants to be with you," Larry offered softly.

Hardened, pain-filled eyes looked up at Larry before returning to the dog sitting comfortably before him.

"I can't imagine why," Sam muttered.

"Sam," Larry continued, "just like Cody wants to be with you, God wants to be with you even more. He loves you, Sam. He always has. And even if you can't love yourself, or forgive yourself, he can."

Sam stared at Larry, his eyes shadowed by anger and cynicism.

And yet there was a hint of something else—something that hadn't been there before: a flicker of hope.

"That he does," Sister Agnes agreed.

The elderly woman rose from her seat, thanked Larry and Susan for coming to visit and for the groceries. She walked over to Cody and patted him. "You're a good boy, Cody."

She then turned to Larry. "I'm going to stay behind and talk to Sam about our dinner plans, but I don't want to keep you folks any longer. Thank you greatly for your kindness."

Larry knew that he and Susan had been dismissed, and he didn't mind at all. Susan hugged Agnes and Larry patted Sam's shoulder.

"Thank you for coming," Sam muttered. The words were spoken in a gruff whisper, but four words had never sounded sweeter to Larry.

🐾

Several days later, Larry opened an email from Pastor Matthew with the text from the therapy dog ministry announcement for him to review. Larry had written the short blurb, the church's administrative assistant had edited it, and Pastor Matthew had reviewed it and sent it back to Larry to sign off on. Once approved, it would be printed in the upcoming Sunday bulletin, as well as listed under the "Ministries" tab on the church website.

> New ministry opportunity for people who love dogs and who love to serve and spread God's message of love and hope into the community. Interested? Contact Larry Randolph to learn how you can get involved in a new therapy dog ministry.

As Larry hit the send button to give his approval to Matthew, his cell phone rang.

"Is this Larry Randolph?" a gravelly male voice asked.

"It sure is."

"My name is Carlos. I live next door to Sam over at Tall Pines. He, uh, he told me about your dog and . . . well . . . uh, do you think you could bring your dog to visit me sometime? I can't afford one of my own, but I sure would . . . well . . . I'd sure like to have one come over."

Larry took Carlos's information and said he and Cody would be happy to visit the following week.

A few hours later Larry's phone rang again. This time a boisterous female voice asked if she was talking to Mr. Larry. Her name was Novie, and she had been at Sister Agnes's house the previous week for dinner.

"Agnes had all sorts of food on her table. We ain't eaten like that in a long time. She said you brought her that food for her to share. That was right kind of you. She also said you have some dogs you've been bringin' around to people out here, and well, I had dogs my whole life and miss 'em right much. Agnes said to give you a call and maybe you could bring a dog to visit me too?"

Larry wrote down Novie's number and address and told her he would be in touch soon to arrange a visit.

He opened his weekly planner and glanced at the upcoming week. Client meetings, proposals to finalize, portfolios to review, a work dinner to discuss the effects the slowing economy was having on their business; visits to Agnes, Shirley, Sam, Carlos, and now Novie; a video call with his daughters; and a date with Susan at Home Depot to pick out yet another paint color for their bathroom walls. How was he going to manage such a full week?

Susan walked into their office, ran her hand over Larry's shoulders, and squeezed.

"You look tense," she observed. "Anything I can do?"

Larry placed his hand over hers. "Just pray we get some takers on our ad in the church bulletin. We're going to need some help. Soon."

CHAPTER FIVE

"Ready, Cody?" Larry asked as the dog leapt from the SUV.

Cody looked up at Larry with his usual happy-go-lucky expression—mouth open, tongue hanging from the side, ears raised. He was the picture of readiness. And although the VA hospital campus they had just pulled into was far larger and more spread out than Larry had anticipated, he was ready too—since the moment Brooke had called with the idea.

"There's a huge need for alternative and supplemental services right now," she had told Larry and Susan the previous week. "In the seven years I've been working at the VA, I can't remember having so many patients with such severe physical and emotional injuries. We have two therapy dog teams that make occasional visits, but I really think this could be a great place for you guys to come with Cody. And I'm not just saying that because I'd get to see him at work," she added with a laugh.

Larry had agreed without hesitation. He trusted Brooke's opinion—both because she was family, and because she was a gifted social worker. But even more than that, Larry believed that he, Susan, and Cody could bring comfort, encouragement, and hope to men and women who had given so much of themselves for others.

"I'll arrange a meeting for you with Cathy Marshall, the director of recreational therapy. The meeting shouldn't take long, but the process of becoming a certified volunteer at the VA can take quite a while."

Brooke advised them about the vaccines and boosters they would need, and about the physicals, orientation, and paperwork they would have to complete. Once she was finished, Susan turned the conversation away from their VA plans.

"Now that all the business is out of the way," she said, "how did your doctor's appointment go? And how are you feeling, sweetheart?"

"It went really well, Mom. And I'm feeling a lot better. The morning sickness has eased up, and I'm starting to feel less tired during the day. Oh, and we got to hear the baby's heartbeat again. I could listen to that sound all day."

Susan squeezed Larry's arm. He knew that she could hardly wait to hold her first biological grandchild. Susan was a fabulous grandmother to Heather's and Kristy's children. Gib and Duncan had been toddlers when she and Larry married—and even though most people couldn't believe Susan was old enough to have grandchildren, she had stepped right into the role of doting grandmother. Then a few years later, Heather and David welcomed sweet Marlowe to the family, followed by her brother Beckett. Susan adored each one. And now she would get to experience the joy of seeing her own child become a parent.

At the same time God was growing a baby in Brooke, he was growing a ministry through Larry and Susan.

"Father, please bless, protect, and grow both our ministry and Brooke's baby according to your perfect will," he prayed. "And thank you that there's no morning sickness involved in creating a therapy dog ministry."

"I had no idea the VA hospital was this big," Susan said, bringing Larry back to the present.

"Me either."

Larry straightened Cody's vest. He wanted to be sure Cody looked the part of professional therapy dog. Granted, he had been serving at the Tall Pines retirement center for two months now, and at the ManorCare Nursing and Rehabilitation Center for the past three weeks. But this was one of the largest veterans' hospitals in the southeastern United States. Larry wanted to represent the ministry well, and he hoped this would be the beginning of a strong partnership with them.

"He looks great, and so do you," Susan assured her husband as the three of them walked into the hospital and headed to the recreational director's office.

"You must be Cathy," Larry said when a friendly looking brunette in her mid-thirties opened the door. "We're Larry and Susan Randolph, and this is Cody."

Cathy welcomed them into her office. "I've heard a lot about you from Brooke. And I've heard *a whole lot* about you," she said to Cody.

Cody leaned against her leg, looked up at her, and offered her his paw.

"Yep, you are going to make a lot of friends here," Cathy chuckled.

Cathy filled in Larry and Susan about the numerous services they offered veterans—including their own trauma center, spinal cord care, rehabilitation facilities, psychiatric services, and hospice care. She gave them a campus map and a new volunteer packet, and pointed out the vaccines they would need.

"Given the seriousness of some of the medical issues our patients are facing, you'll need to be up-to-date on your DPT, flu, and hepatitis vaccines, and tested routinely for tuberculosis. Once those are completed, we'll schedule your orientation classes, and you should be good to go. All in all, it will take about a month to get through the process."

Larry felt like he had been trying to drink from a fire hydrant. The amount of information and steps required to serve at the VA hospital felt overwhelming. And yet, there was no question in his mind that they would complete each and every one.

"Are you ready for a tour?" Cathy took them through the spinal cord and intensive care units and the rehab therapy rooms, then to the brain injury floor, the hospice-care wing and several inpatient hospital floors. They didn't linger in any one place, but everywhere they went, men and women stopped to look at Cody. Larry noticed that several grimaces turned to smiles as the fun-loving dog wagged his tail in anticipation of meeting so many new friends.

After thanking Cathy and saying goodbye, Larry and Susan headed back to their car with Cody. Just as Larry was about to open the back door of the SUV for Cody, a young woman approached them. Her cheeks were flushed, her eyes were puffy, and her clothes were rumpled and worn. She hesitated. Larry thought perhaps she was going to ask for money, which he would have gladly given her. But that wasn't what she was looking for.

"May I, um . . . pet your dog for a second?"

"Of course," Larry and Susan answered in unison.

The woman knelt in front of Cody, leaned her head against his, and inhaled a shaky breath. Cody scooted closer to the woman, who wrapped her arms around him and began to sob.

"Oh, sweetheart," Susan said, placing her hand on the woman's trembling back.

"I have to . . ." A sob broke her words. "I have to . . . go in there . . . and say . . . how am I going to say goodbye? I don't know how . . . I can't."

Cody pressed his forehead to the sobbing woman's. Larry didn't know if she was speaking about her husband, a parent, or another loved one. He didn't need to know any details because God already did. So Larry offered her all he could.

"May I pray for you?"

She nodded, keeping her head against Cody's.

"Dear heavenly Father, we don't know the circumstances surrounding this situation, but we do know that you are aware of everything, and that you are the God of comfort, love, and peace. We ask you to bring the right words to the mind and heart of this precious young lady as she offers her love and compassion to this one she is heartbroken to say goodbye to. We pray that she will feel your love as she spends time with this dear soul. May she experience and express the hope of Jesus and may this bring comfort and peace in this difficult situation. Amen."

"Thank you," the woman whispered. Then she touched her head to Cody's one last time. "Thank you."

"Poor thing," Susan said, opening the rear driver's side door for Cody as the young woman walked away.

Larry checked his watch. They had only twenty minutes to get to the ManorCare nursing home for their previously scheduled visit.

He had reached out to the facilities director—as well as several other nursing home directors—after his meeting with Pastor Matthew. All but one had welcomed the idea of him bringing Cody and other therapy dogs to visit their residents. Larry hoped to be able to schedule other visits at even more facilities, but they would need help to do so. Thankfully, he had already received three phone calls from people interested in learning more about the ministry. If God wanted them to reach more people, he would provide more people—and dogs.

Larry and Susan were quiet on the drive to ManorCare. They had made enough visits to know that sometimes a brief silence can help reset the heart and mind. Larry also suspected that Susan was praying for the young woman from the VA hospital—just as he was doing.

They were only five minutes late and quickly fell into an easy rhythm with the guests. Aside from visiting two residents in their rooms, they spent most of their hour in the common area, visiting with those who expressed interest in meeting a therapy dog. Larry loved the way their faces lit up when they noticed Cody.

"Hi, pup!" a bright-eyed woman in a wheelchair called out.

Cody walked directly to her and placed his head on her lap. Larry and Susan greeted the woman and said how glad they were to see her. A man, hunched over a tray attached to his wheelchair, pulled his hand back and forth in an awkward "come here" motion. It seemed difficult for him to raise his head so Larry bent down to say hello and asked if he would like to see Cody. The man bobbed his head slightly, so Larry brought Cody over to sit in his line of vision, with his head close enough for the man to touch. A nurse discreetly wiped a tear from her eye, telling Susan that the man had Alzheimer's and had been "virtually unreachable" for days—until now.

Cody stayed by the man's side until the dinner announcement was made, the signal for Larry, Susan, and Cody to end the day's visit and take Cody home.

"How can I feel so full and so empty at the same time?" Susan wondered aloud.

Larry knew exactly what she meant. And as Cody lay down in the back seat with a louder than usual sigh, he suspected the dog did too. Acting on a whim, Larry drove past the exit for Brooke's house and headed for a dog-friendly beach. Cody's ears perked up the moment Larry pulled into a parking space and grabbed a Frisbee from the back of the SUV. When Cody's door was opened, he bolted from the car so fast, Larry nearly dropped the end of the leash and had to run to keep up with him.

Susan took her shoes off and headed straight for the water. Cody tugged Larry forward, but Larry told him to "sit" and unhooked his leash. Cody ran to Susan, bumped her hand with his nose, then raced back to Larry and sat so dutifully it looked as if he was awaiting to be knighted.

"You sure do look regal when you want me to throw your Frisbee," Larry joked.

For the next half hour, Susan walked in the surf while Larry played Frisbee with Cody. The retriever was in heaven. His tail wagged nonstop, his tongue hung from his mouth, and his eyes never left the flying disc. The impromptu salt air–saturated fun was exactly what all of them had needed. Taking care of themselves, and ensuring they weren't trying to pour out energy they didn't have, would need to become a vital part of their routine—and any ministry training they did in the future. Larry knew self-care and canine care were key components to their success.

Forty-five minutes later, they packed up to head to Brooke and Bryan's house. Larry glanced in the rearview mirror at the sleeping dog curled up on a beach towel in the back seat.

Cody sensed when they were getting close, so there was no need to wake him up. When Larry opened the car door, Cody leaped out and shook himself from nose to tail, ran up the walk, and pawed at the front door to get in. His whole body wiggled with his wagging tail when Brooke opened the door.

"There's my boy . . . my wet boy?" She chuckled, looking at Susan for an explanation.

"It was my idea," Larry admitted. "A spur-of-the-moment trip to the beach. We'll be more than happy to give Cody a bath before we leave."

Brooke waved them off. "Cody was due for a bath anyway. Bryan and I will take care of that." Susan gave Brooke a distinct "mom look." Brooke laughed and said, "I mean, I'll sit back with my feet up and watch while Bryan does it."

"That's my girl."

CHAPTER SIX

THE FOLLOWING SUNDAY, Larry and Susan arrived at church twenty minutes earlier than usual.

"Any sign of them?" Susan asked Larry.

Larry chuckled. "I've never seen you this excited—or impatient—to see them." But the truth was, he was just as anxious for them to arrive. This wasn't a typical Sunday for either couple. A few moments later, Brooke and Bryan were standing beside them.

"Cody!" Larry exclaimed.

The dog jumped into Larry's open arms. "We've been a lot of places together, but never to church before, huh, buddy? Thank you both for bringing Cody today. When Pastor Matthew said he wanted to formally introduce the therapy dog ministry, I knew it would be a special day, but when he suggested bringing Cody to the service, I knew it would be an extra special day. No better way to show people what this ministry is about than letting them meet its canine ambassador. "What do you think, Cody? Is it time to go to work?"

Cody answered with an excited bark. For the next twenty minutes, Larry and Cody greeted people entering the church lobby. The reactions varied—delight, confusion, and one look of annoyance. But the majority of people were curious and approached the Golden Retriever.

"Why is that dog in church?" a little boy asked.

Cody sniffed the boy's pants, then his hands. Larry had no doubt Cody was searching for remnants of his breakfast.

"This is Cody, and he wanted to come to church to meet some new friends and help people know that God loves them," Larry replied.

"I know that God loves me," the boy said.

"I am so glad to hear that. Since you know how much God loves you, you can be like Cody and help other people learn that God loves them too."

"Okay!" the boy agreed enthusiastically before darting off into the worship center.

Larry talked with several other people before joining Susan, Brooke, and Bryan in the last row of seats inside. Cody curled up at Larry's feet, but when the congregation stood to sing, Cody jumped up and looked expectantly at Larry. At the end of the third song, Cody lay back down and fell fast asleep with his head on Larry's foot during Pastor Matthew's sermon, certainly not a critique of the morning message.

After the closing song, Matthew invited Larry to come forward.

"Folks, I get to make a very special introduction today," he said, as Cody bounded toward him. "Most of you know Larry Randolph, and it is my joy to introduce my new friend, Cody. Larry and Cody have started a brand-new therapy dog ministry and are looking to add some volunteers, so I asked him to tell you about it. And since the ministry is all about bringing God's love to people through wonderful dogs like Cody, I asked Larry to bring him too."

Larry spent the next five minutes explaining his vision for the ministry. He described what the visits looked like and the simple requirements of participants in the program—that all volunteers express a faith and trust in Jesus and be willing to share God's love with others, and that all dogs be current on their vaccinations and pass the Canine Good Citizen test.

"My phone number and email address are printed on the back of the church bulletin, so if you have any questions or would like to join us, please reach out to me. I would love to talk with you. Thank you so much."

After the closing prayer, as people began to leave, Larry was approached by his and Susan's dear friends Charlie and Jane Palmer.

"So how is retirement treating you?" Larry asked Charlie.

"I should have done it years ago," he answered. "But it sounds like you're gearing up for a career change."

"Oh, I don't know about that. Right now, the ministry doesn't require too much time or effort. Our biggest need at this point is more people and dogs. Maybe someday I could see it requiring more of my time. The truth is," he leaned a little closer to Charlie, "I love it. I love talking with people. I love working with Cody. And I love telling people how much God loves them. To be honest, it doesn't even feel like work."

"Well, you've sold us!" Charlie exclaimed.

Jane jumped in. "We've been part of a different therapy dog group with our German Shepherd, Van Gogh, and we love it."

"It's wonderful to watch people connect with him," Charlie continued, "but we've been feeling like we want to do more."

Larry's heart swelled with gratitude. "We would be honored and delighted to have you join us. Let's talk more over dinner later this week."

Larry and Cody were also stopped by a middle-aged woman named Annette who expressed interest in volunteering with her black-haired terrier, Ditto. Several other people said they would be praying for the ministry, a few said they would be making a donation to the ministry through the church fund, and a schoolteacher named Gloria said she would like to join with her beagle, Elvis.

Larry was overwhelmed by God's provision. When he got to the parking lot, Pastor Matthew was waiting for him.

"Larry, before you go, I wanted to mention something. When you explained that you want to bring God's love and comfort to people, it occurred to me that you are describing the role of a chaplain. Have you ever considered becoming a certified chaplain?"

Larry shook his head.

"Not only would it give you access to training and a community of chaplains, but it could also open a lot of doors for you and the ministry—especially when it comes to providing support during local and national tragedies. If you'd like, I can send you some information about the process. And I would be honored to have our church sponsor you—that is, if it's something you would like to pursue."

Larry was deeply touched by Pastor Matthew's words and his belief in him.

"Thank you so much, Pastor," he replied, finding it hard to

articulate what was on his heart. "I will definitely give this some prayer and thought."

A few weeks later, Larry and Susan were again on their way to the VA hospital with Cody. Thankfully, they had added several more volunteers to the ministry, which allowed them to provide therapy dog services across a larger area each week—including a new partnership at a day program for adults called Trinity, which served people with intellectual and developmental challenges.

Larry pulled into the visitor's parking lot at the main VA campus, took a deep breath, and let out an involuntary sigh.

"Are you sure you're feeling up to this today?" Susan asked, motioning to his ankle.

He had started experiencing pain a few weeks earlier. It had started off mild and intermittent, but after a long day of site visits for work followed by therapy dog visits, the pain had become so intense that he had to limp to bed. Thankfully, icing his ankle and keeping it elevated all evening had helped. As had a full dose of ibuprofen.

"I'll be fine," he said. "Compared to the injuries we'll see today, a little ankle pain is nothing."

Susan looked skeptical, and she made him promise to rest his ankle as soon as they got home. The three of them entered the building and headed to the long-term care floor. It was their third time visiting this area of the medical campus where people with debilitating injuries or illnesses received ongoing care.

"Here boy!" an elderly man called out from his room as Cody paraded down the hall.

From the way the sheet lay on the man's bed, Larry could tell the man had lost both legs. And from the way his face lit up and his arms stretched forward, he could also tell the man desperately wanted to pet Cody.

"Hello there, sir," Larry greeted. "I'm Larry Randolph and this is Cody. May we come in?"

The man nodded, and a toothless grin transformed his face into an expression of joy and anticipation.

"Paws up," Larry instructed. Cody went to the side of the bed, stood on his back legs, and put his front paws on the mattress so the man could touch him. Larry was thankful that Cody had learned the new command so quickly, giving bedbound patients the opportunity to interact with the dog.

While Cody charmed the man, Larry learned his name was Mitch and that he was being treated for complications from diabetes. Mitch didn't have any family in the area and seemed to be enjoying the attention he was receiving from his nurses—and now from Cody. When their visit was cut short by the occupational therapist, Larry assured Mitch that they would return in a few days.

Larry and Susan poked their heads into each room, asking the patient if they would like a visit from a therapy dog. Most people said yes, a few declined, and a few others were sleeping. In the room at the end of the hall, a woman was sitting beside the bed where a man lay sleeping. Larry gently knocked on the partially open door and introduced Susan, Cody, and himself.

"We are part of a therapy dog ministry and just wanted to see if you'd like a visit with Cody."

The woman—who appeared to be in her early seventies—discreetly wiped tears from her cheek and nodded. Cody needed no further encouragement. He walked purposefully into the room with his open-mouthed smile and leaned his head against the arm of her chair. She closed her eyes and ran her hand down Cody's back.

In the almost nine months since their first hospital visit with Cody, Larry had gained a better understanding of when to offer prayer and when to simply let Cody offer God's love and nearness to someone. He never wanted to force prayer on anyone or make them feel uncomfortable, but he also wanted people to know that God cared for them and stood ready to help them. More often than not, people—even those who did not share his faith—welcomed his prayers. Larry sensed this woman needed prayer.

"Could we pray with you?" he asked softly. "And for your . . . ?"

"Husband, Charlie," she said, her voice breaking on the last syllable. She cleared her throat, nodded, and then added, "He had some . . . complications—" she cleared her throat again and adjusted her grip on his hand—"after surgery for an abdominal aneurysm. He was just transferred here. But the doctors don't think . . ." she paused and lowered her head.

Cody stretched under the arm of the chair and laid his head on her leg. She sat up and patted him. "I'm Shelba, by the way. The doctors have told us not to get our hopes up. They say Charlie's condition is likely terminal. But my Charlie is a fighter."

She squeezed Charlie's hand, and Larry noticed the man's eyes slowly open. Even though Charlie wasn't fully awake, Shelba introduced him to Larry and Susan—and Cody. Then she stood and pulled her chair back so that Cody could reach the bed. She carefully took Charlie's arm—the one without an IV—and placed it at the edge of the bed so he could feel the dog's soft fur.

"Cody wants to say hi."

Cody nudged Charlie's hand, and Larry could have sworn the

corner of Charlie's lips turned up slightly. His mouth opened in an attempt to speak, but no sound came.

"The journey here was really hard on him," Shelba offered.

"Well, we will let him get the rest he needs, but before we go, we would love to pray with you."

Shelba took hold of Charlie's hand and placed her other hand on Cody's head.

"Father, we thank you for Charlie and Shelba. Thank you for the love they have for each other. Please let them feel the love you have for them—especially now in this difficult time. Fill them with your comfort and your peace, and give them an abundance of hope. Amen."

"Thank you. Will you come again?" Shelba asked.

"We'll be back the day after tomorrow."

Hours later, Larry sat in his home office, trying to finish an assignment for the chaplain program he had started the week before. He was only two assignments into the program but was already grateful to Pastor Matthew for suggesting it. He rubbed the dull pain in his right temple, then adjusted the ice pack on his ankle.

Logging off the chaplain website, he opened the folder on his desk. It was time to switch gears from spiritual needs to real estate investments. But before long, his eyelids grew heavy and his shoulders started to droop.

After leaving the hospital that afternoon, they had dropped Cody off at Brooke's, then raced home to host their church fellowship group. The five couples had been meeting for years to pray and talk about what they were reading in the Bible. Larry normally loved their gatherings, but it had been hard to stay focused this evening. His thoughts kept drifting to Charlie and Shelba and others they had visited. He apologized to the group for feeling distracted, and they graciously prayed that he and Susan and everyone involved in the ministry would feel comforted by God's presence.

But now, as the clock blinked the time of a new day, he felt too weary to focus on his work proposal. He trudged down the dark hallway to the bedroom, set his alarm for 5:00 a.m., and collapsed into bed.

Two days later, Larry and Susan returned to the VA hospital.

"Are you up for a short visit?" Larry asked Shelba.

The older woman greeted them with a bright smile and waved them in. Cody pulled slightly against the leash as he made a beeline for his new friend.

"You look beautiful," Susan observed. "Are you going somewhere?"

Shelba chuckled, smoothed her skirt, and then dismissed her question with a slight shake of her head.

"No. I just always like to look nice for my Charlie."

"Don't let her fool you," a raspy male voice teased. "She just likes to shop."

"Well, hello there!" Larry exclaimed, walking to the opposite side of the bed. "It is so nice to meet you, Charlie. I'm Larry. This is my wife, Susan, and our dog, Cody."

Charlie stretched a thin arm toward Cody.

"Paws up," Larry said, patting the bed.

Cody eagerly complied, lowering his head for Charlie's touch.

"Nice to meet you, Cody," Charlie said, before raising striking blue eyes toward Larry and then over to Susan. "And it's nice to meet you both too. Shelba told me about your last visit. I'm sorry that I was a bit out of it."

Larry patted Charlie on his shoulder. "We're just glad you're feeling a little better today."

"I am," he replied, wincing slightly as he placed his hand on his abdomen. "In fact, I'm sure I'll be up and ready for a steak dinner in no time."

"All he's talked about is steak, steak, steak," Shelba said with a twinkle in her eye. "Leave it to my husband to whisper sweet nothings about a slab of meat instead of me or our daughters."

Charlie reached for her hand. "You and the girls will always have my heart. But my taste buds? Well, that's a different story."

Larry couldn't believe a man in such pain could still have such a wonderful sense of humor. They spent the next fifteen minutes laughing and sharing stories of their grown daughters, while Cody alternated between being petted by Shelba and Charlie. But when Charlie leaned his head back and closed his eyes for a moment, Larry knew it was time to end the visit. Larry prayed with them and they exchanged hugs. As Larry got to the door, Charlie called out, "Next time, feel free to bring me a steak!"

Laughing, Larry had a different proposal. "How about when you get out of here, we go to Bern's Steak House, and I'll get you the biggest steak they have."

"You have a deal!" Charlie agreed.

Larry chuckled, but his heart dropped at the sound of Charlie's cough. "God, please let us be able to share that steak someday soon," he prayed silently.

After visiting five more patients in long-term care, the trio went to the rehabilitation floor, then made the long walk to the spinal cord injury building, where they met with several more

patients in various stages of recovery. Larry and Susan were starting to get tired, but Cody never slowed down. He gave every
nurse, patient, doctor, visitor, and hospital employee his winning
Cody smile. And his wagging tail made almost everyone smile in
return—even the families they met on the hospice floor and in
the trauma center.

Larry was overwhelmed with the severity of injuries and dis-
figurements he witnessed. The need was so great—and the emotional burden so heavy. But Cody never faltered. He greeted each
person with the same energy and excitement as the one before,
eagerly receiving pats and touches from bandaged hands or rubbing against the legs of patients without arms. Cody welcomed
hugs from grieving family members and complied with requests
for handshakes at the nurses' stations.

"Cody, you were made for this," Larry said, patting the dog
after visiting with residents of Cove Community Living Center,
the VA hospital's nursing home facility. As they headed toward
the exit, Larry noticed a man and woman in the exercise room.
The man was riding a stationary bike, and the woman, who Larry
assumed was an aide or caregiver, stood close beside him, with her
hand on his back.

"Hi there," Larry said as he and Susan and Cody walked into
the room. "I can see you're hard at work, but I was wondering if
we might interrupt for a minute?"

The man's head swayed, and he made a series of unintelligible
sounds. The woman leaned toward him and spoke softly. Larry
heard the words *visitors*, *dog*, and *nice*. She helped the man off the
bike, took his hand, and led him to Larry and Susan.

"I'm Larry, and this is my wife, Susan," Larry said, extending
his hand.

The woman placed the man's hand in Larry's.

"This is Bernard. And I am his aide, Donna."

Bernard made a series of sounds, but Larry couldn't discern any words. "Mr. Bernard is blind and nonverbal, but he likes to meet new friends."

"Well, we are very glad to meet you, Bernard," Larry said, patting the man on the back. "And our dog, Cody, is very happy to meet you too."

Bernard quickly withdrew his hand and started to shuffle backwards. His vocalizations sounded troubled; it was clear he was becoming agitated. Donna put her arm around the man's shoulders to calm him.

"Bernard, you don't have to touch the dog. He's on a leash and is standing behind Larry. He's a big dog, but he looks friendly and gentle. He has long, soft fur, dark eyes, and a long tongue."

Larry smiled as Bernard stuck out his own tongue.

"Would you like to touch the dog?" Donna asked.

Bernard's head bobbed up and down, and he raised his arm for Donna to lead him, but Larry could tell he was nervous.

"Cody, sit."

"I am going to put your hand on Cody's back, okay, Bernard?" Donna asked.

When Bernard made no objection, she slowly lowered his hand. At first, Bernard jerked it away, but Cody didn't move a muscle and when Bernard realized he was in no danger, he laid his hand on Cody's back and smiled. Bernard moved his hand up and down, seeming to enjoy the way Cody's fur felt between his fingers. His vocalizations became louder and more exuberant the longer he petted the dog. After several minutes of sitting still, Cody stood and touched his nose to Bernard's hand. The simple action brought what Larry could only describe as a guttural squeal of joy from Bernard.

"Bernard, we're so glad to know you," he said. "You are so loved—by God, by Donna, by Cody, and by us. Thank you for letting us say hello. Would it be okay if we bring Cody back again soon to see you?"

Bernard's entire upper body bobbed in agreement, and his joyful sounds followed them all the way to the lobby.

CHAPTER SEVEN

"What time do we need to be there?" Susan asked, nervously chewing her bottom lip.

"They want to start right at nine," Larry replied, with a quick glance over his shoulder as he merged onto Gunn Highway. He had barely reached the speed limit when traffic slowed and came to a standstill. Susan exhaled loudly.

"We're never going to make it."

Larry glanced at the dashboard clock. At this rate, they would have just enough time to load Cody in the car and get back on the road. Normally they spent several minutes with Brooke and five-month-old Luke before leaving with Cody. But today they were participating in a clinical study to measure brain-wave and blood-flow activity in comatose patients exposed to a therapy dog. They needed to get there on time.

Larry wished they had left home a little earlier—and that they lived closer to Brooke.

Maybe it's time to get our own dog and train it for this work. But as quickly as the thought came, Larry dismissed it. After all, Cody was clearly meant to be a therapy dog. Still . . .

Father, if you want us to get another dog for the ministry, will you make that abundantly clear? For now, I just want to thank you—once again—for Cody and for the work you are doing through him. And Lord, if it's your will, please get us to the study on time.

"Thank you, Lord," Larry said aloud as they pulled into the parking lot with four minutes to spare and hurried Cody to the neurology department. Cathy Marshall, who was part of the team overseeing the study, greeted them outside the trauma ward.

"Thank you both so much for helping us with this. And thank you for helping us, too, Cody! The neurologist would like to put Cody in bed next to our patient, Mark, who has been in a comatose state for weeks," Cathy explained. "Mark will be connected to several different monitors, which will alert us to any changes in his blood-flow or brain-wave activity."

She paused for a moment. "Will Cody be okay under those conditions?"

Larry nodded. Thankfully, he had already gotten Cody used to being picked up and placed in bed next to a patient, instead of him *jumping into a bed* with a patient. It was a necessary adjustment after an unfortunate—and at the time horrifying—incident when Cody had jumped up on a patient's bed and inadvertently pulled out his IV. The bleeding patient had waved the incident off with a chuckle, but the nurse had been less than amused, and Larry had wanted the floor to open up and swallow him whole. From that moment on, Larry not only lifted Cody onto the bed himself but included the story as a cautionary tale when training new volunteers.

"Cody will be just fine," he assured her. "May we ask a little about Mark's background? Or is that confidential?"

"No, I'm glad you asked," Cathy smiled. "Mark is an Air Force pilot who sustained a traumatic brain injury when his plane was shot down over Iraq. He and his wife have only been married a short time, and she spends every day here with him. She's hopeful that today's study will show an increase in Mark's brain activity, but given the severity of his injuries, we don't expect much of a measurable increase."

Susan placed her hand in Larry's and squeezed, an unspoken signal that she was praying—undoubtedly asking God to intervene in this heartbreaking situation.

"Are you ready?" Cathy asked.

Larry and Susan nodded. Cody raised his ears, wagged his tail, and stepped forward. Cathy led them into Mark's hospital room. After briefly introducing Dr. Perry—the neurologist leading the study—and the nurses and technicians helping him, Cathy introduced them to Mark's wife, Julie.

"Thank you for coming," the young woman said.

The dark circles under her eyes tore at Larry's heart. She should be out on this warm summer day, enjoying a nice breakfast with her husband—not sitting vigil at his bedside. *Oh Father, encourage and comfort this young woman today.*

"We are so honored to be here," Susan said, placing her hand on Julie's shoulder. "And also so very sorry for the situation that brought us here."

Julie pulled a tissue from her pocket and mouthed *thank you.*

Meanwhile, a technician adjusted several of the wires connected to Mark's head, chest, and arms.

"You can go ahead and put Cody beside him," she instructed, pointing to Mark's left side. "Once he's in position, I'll make sure the monitors are in the right places and we'll get started."

Larry lifted Cody, who never felt heavy, even at eighty-five pounds. If anything, lifting him up to place him beside someone in need felt like an act of worship.

"Do what God made you to do," Larry whispered.

He positioned Cody so that his head was facing Mark, and his warm body was against Mark's torso and upper leg. A nurse then placed Mark's arm on Cody's side and moved his hand back and forth slowly through Cody's fur. Cody gently nudged Mark's shoulder. After getting no reaction, the dog exhaled deeply and laid his head on Mark's chest, near his shoulder.

Monitors beeped, machines buzzed, and the intercom in the hallway relayed messages at a rapid-fire pace, but Cody was unaffected by the cacophony of sounds in the trauma ward and remained perfectly still.

Larry and Susan had made many visits to the trauma floor with Cody over the past several months, and the dog had been calm and steady for each visit. But observing him now—with his head on Mark's chest, his soulful eyes watching his new friend, and his rhythmic breaths causing Mark's arm to gently rise and fall—Larry's eyes burned with respect and gratitude for the dog. The intuitive, gentle canine's presence offered comfort to everyone in the room.

Julie stood at the foot of Mark's bed, hands clasped under her chin, and tears spilling down her cheeks.

"Mark's always loved dogs," she whispered. "We were going to get one when he got back from . . ." She shook her head against a silent sob and reached for a tissue. Susan squeezed her arm.

"We're all set." Dr. Perry flipped a switch on the machine closest to him and began watching the screen, while a technician continued to move Mark's hand through Cody's fur.

"May we talk to him?" Larry asked, unsure if that would skew the results.

"Absolutely," Cathy answered. "We're looking at the effects of therapy dog visits as a whole, so please treat this as you would any other visit."

That was all Larry needed to hear. Regardless of whether or not Mark could reply, he believed the man needed to hear what everyone needs to hear—that they are loved and that their lives matter.

"Hello there, Mark," he spoke quietly into the man's left ear. "We are so honored to be here and have loved getting to know Julie. We know you're so proud of her. She sure does love you a lot." Larry heard her whisper *more than anything.* "We hear you like dogs, so we brought Cody with us today. He's a Golden Retriever, and he sure does like you. In fact, he hasn't stopped looking at you since we got here." The technician continued to move Mark's arm back and forth along Cody's side as Larry spoke. "Cody feels very safe with you, Mark."

"Is that . . ." Julie's words trailed off as her head went back and forth between the screen and her husband. "Is he . . . ?" Her bottom lip started quivering as hopeful tears filled her deep-blue eyes.

Dr. Perry nodded. "It's too soon to say for sure, but that line," he pointed at a rising line on the monitor, "is indicating a slight increase in blood flow. And that one," he pointed to another screen with lines that resembled an EKG, "is recording what appears to be a little bit of brain-wave activity."

A sob escaped Julie's lips, and she grabbed her husband's foot. "Baby, I'm here. I love you so much. Keep fighting! I know you're there. I know it."

"Yes, we are definitely detecting some activity," a technician said with surprise and delight.

"We'll need some time to analyze the data and write up a report," Dr. Perry cautioned, "but I'm very encouraged by these preliminary findings." He put his hand on Cody's back. "Good dog."

Cathy caught Larry's eye and mouthed *thank you*.

Larry nodded. The moment felt too sacred—too holy—for words.

They remained in silence for several minutes while Mark's arm rested on Cody and the machines kept recording. An hour after walking into Mark's room, Dr. Perry said they had enough information for the study.

Julie walked around the bed, nuzzled Cody and spoke softly to him as he laid his head on her shoulder.

When she stood up, Larry carefully lifted Cody off the bed and placed him back on the floor. Cody had no idea of the impact he had just made. But it was something Larry—and he suspected Julie—would never forget.

🐾

Two weeks later, Larry dropped Susan off at Brooke's to watch Luke while he and Cody made some visits.

Their first stop was the newly opened Suncoast Kids Place, where grieving children and teens could receive support and safely process their feelings.

"*Oof!* Slow down there a little," Larry said, as Cody bounded from the back seat.

Larry stopped at the curb to stretch his ankle. He was paying the price today for walking around the hospital campus for three hours yesterday. Pastor Matthew met them at the door.

Larry had tried to brace himself for the grief he knew those who came to Suncoast would be experiencing, and yet, there was no way he could have prepared himself for the heartbreak he saw on a young mother's face as she walked through the doors holding two young children by the hand. She introduced herself as Angela and nodded to two-year-old Robbie, who was hiding behind her leg, and three-year-old Savannah, who stretched out her arms to Cody. The children had recently lost their newborn sister, Haley—and the grief-stricken mother had called the church for help.

A trained volunteer took the children over to a play area, while Matthew and Larry led Angela to one of the counseling rooms. Normally, it was children who received services at Suncoast, but it was clear Angela needed support and a safe place to process her heartbreak.

"We are so very sorry for your loss," Matthew said softly.

The young mother sat silently on the sofa, and Cody walked over and laid his head on her lap. Angela wrapped her arms around Cody as she wept, and Larry and Matthew prayed softly.

When her tears began to subside, she said, "They were so excited about having a baby sister. Robbie chattered all day to my belly, and Savannah listened to the baby with her toy stethoscope." Tears trailed down her cheeks as the sweet memory turned painful. "They jumped up and down when we brought Haley home from the hospital. They didn't want to let her out of their sight. *I* never should have let her out of my sight." She clung to Cody as if he alone could keep her from drowning in a sea of pain. "I put her down for a nap and . . ."

Larry knelt beside her.

"She was gone when I went to check on her. Just gone." Her sobs were silent now, as if she had no energy left to cry.

She shared a little more about her baby girl and about the dark days she'd faced since her death. Larry and Matthew listened far more than they spoke, and then they prayed for Angela, her husband, Tom, and for Robbie and Savannah to sense God's comfort.

After taking a moment to collect herself, Angela asked if Robbie and Savannah could see Cody.

"That's why we're here," Larry said, leading Cody toward the children.

Savannah smiled at Cody, but Robbie ran to his mother's arms.

"It's okay, baby," she said, hugging him tightly. "Cody is mama's friend."

Robbie's chubby index finger touched Angela's cheek and then pointed at Cody.

"Mama fend?" he asked.

Angela nodded.

"Van-nah's fend?"

"Yes, Cody is Savannah's friend too," Angela assured him.

"Hay-yee fend?" His little voice asked.

Larry could hear Angela's sharp intake of air.

She closed her eyes and smiled a sad smile. "Yes, baby, Cody is Haley's friend too."

Robbie climbed down from Angela's arms and stood before Cody. He watched his sister pet Cody's back and mimicked her motions.

"Van-nah's fend! Aw-bbie's fend!" The two-year-old's giggles filled the room as Cody rolled over and offered him his belly.

CHAPTER EIGHT

"Oh, Larry, I'm so glad we did this!" Susan exclaimed, as he steered their SUV into the gravel parking lot of the bed-and-breakfast they had booked for the weekend. "I didn't realize how much I needed to get away."

The drive to St. Augustine had taken only three hours, but it felt like they were a world away from work, house, and ministry responsibilities. Larry loved the work he did. But there was no denying the toll it was taking, on both his emotions and his body. His ankle pain was almost constant now, and he fell into bed most nights empty and exhausted.

Their occasional trips to the beach with Cody to play and enjoy a sunset always helped refuel their spirits. But as the ministry—which now consisted of twelve volunteer teams—approached its one-year anniversary, Larry and Susan were averaging twenty hours a week making visits, with at least ten of those hours spent at the VA hospital. A little self-care was definitely in order.

The trip refreshed both of them. At breakfast, their conversation turned to imagining what God might have in store for the ministry's second year. Larry planned to retire from real estate and transition into full-time ministry. Susan wondered aloud how many more volunteers would sign up, while Larry envisioned teams being deployed to offer comfort and support to those affected by hurricanes, tornados, or fires.

He also wondered if he and Susan would have a therapy dog of their own so that Cody could spend more time with Luke. But once again, Larry pushed the thought from his mind. He couldn't imagine another dog as well-suited for this work as Cody.

God, once again I give this worry to you. Please provide for this ministry as you see fit.

"Oh, by the way," Susan said, "we'll need to order more vests when we get home."

"Are you two in an act? Or do you just really like vests?" The owner of the bed-and-breakfast chuckled as she approached to refill their water glasses.

"Neither, thankfully," Larry replied smiling. "The vests are for therapy dogs."

The woman, who introduced herself as "Katie, the bed-and-breakfast lady," said she often took her dogs to visit a nearby nursing home.

Susan, in turn, told Katie about the different places the ministry's therapy dogs visited, including the work they were doing at the hospital. As they continued to talk, it became clear that Katie shared their faith and greatly admired the way they worked with the dogs to bring God's love to people.

"It's like you have a whole group of canines for Christ," Katie said.

Larry and Susan's eyes met. *That's it!* A new ministry year and a new ministry name. Three simple words that perfectly summed up their mission statement: *Canines for Christ.*

🐾

A week after Larry and Susan arrived home, they were leaving the veterans' hospital with Cody one day when Cathy Marshall caught them.

"I'm so glad I saw you," she said, leading them into a quiet hallway. "I wanted to show you the final results of the neurological study you participated in."

She flipped to the final page of a folder filled with charts, graphs, and data. "Thirty percent! We measured a thirty percent increase in blood flow from Mark's brain when he was touching Cody! This study clearly demonstrates the positive effects of pet therapy on even the most brain-injured patients."

Larry knew that the study had gone well. He'd felt the sacredness of the moment and seen the optimistic looks on the faces in the room. But now, seeing concrete data . . . he had never felt more proud and humbled at the same time.

No sooner did Cathy step away than a woman Larry and Susan had never seen approached them.

"Hi, I'm a nurse here, and I've heard all about the awesome work you are doing with your dog, and I was wondering . . ." She paused to pet Cody, then said, "My friend Denise breeds white English Labradors, and she just welcomed a new litter. Denise is a Christian, and I was telling her about your ministry, and she would really like to support you guys, and well . . . I know you already have a dog, and from what I hear he's a rock star around here, but if you'd like another one she'd like to offer you one of her puppies."

The woman handed Susan a business card. "Here's Denise's number. Just give her a call if you're interested. She'd love to meet you." Before Larry and Susan could even respond, the nurse's pager went off, and she headed toward the trauma unit. "Just think about it. No pressure. Gotta run, bye!"

Larry and Susan looked at each other and said in unison, "Someone wants to give us a puppy?"

They walked out of the hospital, loaded Cody in the back seat, and drove him home in contemplative silence.

"There's my boy!" Brooke called out from the front door, Luke on her hip.

His chubby little legs started kicking the moment he saw Cody, and when the dog licked his foot, Luke squealed in delight.

🐾

Three days later, Denise Griffith placed a wriggling white puppy in Larry's arms.

"This is the little girl I wanted you to meet," she said, as the four-week-old puppy licked Larry's cheek. "She is one of the calmest puppies we've ever had, with the sweetest temperament. When Barbara told me about your ministry, I felt like God was saying, 'This dog belongs to me.'"

Larry held the puppy up to his face, so they were nose to nose. Her eyes were a deep blue-gray, though Denise said they would likely change to brown over the next few days. The puppy watched Larry with an intensity that surprised him. It felt like she could see right into his soul. *How could eyes that haven't yet finished developing hold such wisdom?*

The puppy licked Larry's nose. He cradled her in his arms and looked at Susan, who was clearly as smitten with the precious little puppy as he was.

"She's perfect," Larry said. "But I imagine such a beautiful dog, from such a wonderful-looking place—" he nodded toward manicured lawns, the horse pasture in the distance, and the large, climate-controlled dog kennels—"costs quite a bit of money. I know Barbara said you wanted to *give* us a puppy, but surely we need to pay you something?"

Denise shook her head. "No, you don't. And yes, my puppies usually sell for $1,500 to $2,000, but like I told you, God said this was his puppy. And with the work you are doing through Canines for Christ, I know this little girl was meant for you. So if you'd like her, then you can come back in four weeks and take her home."

Larry was speechless. The phrase *grace upon grace* went through his mind.

"Thank you, Denise," Susan said. "We're overwhelmed by your generosity. And so very grateful to you."

"We are indeed," Larry added, with tears in his eyes.

Larry kissed the puppy's tiny brown nose. "I'll see you soon, little one."

When they were back in the SUV, Susan asked, "What are you going to name her?"

Larry didn't even need to think about it. Her name was as clear as if God himself had spoken it aloud from the heavens.

"Her name is Grace."

CHAPTER NINE

"Welcome, Gracie! This is your home now."

Larry was relieved at how well the eight-week-old Lab had handled the hour-long car ride from Denise's kennels in Weeki Wachee back to Tampa. Susan drove and Larry held Gracie, who tucked her head into the crook of his arm and fell asleep. She stayed so still Susan joked that surely Denise had given them an extremely realistic-looking stuffed animal by mistake.

When Susan pulled into the driveway and turned off the car, Gracie raised her head. Larry carried her to the grass so she could relieve herself and then took her into her new home. He gave her the grand tour, telling Gracie the name of each room and its function.

The final stop was the kitchen. "You will love this room. This is where we eat. Susan and I eat at that table. And you will eat right over here," he said, setting her in front of two stainless-steel bowls on the floor.

Gracie looked at the water bowl and then at Larry. He dipped his finger in the water and gently touched her nose. She lowered her head and took a long drink. When she lifted her head, water dribbled from her chin. *Note to self: Get a waterproof mat to put under the bowls*, thought Larry.

Gracie started exploring her new environment, sniffing everything she could reach—the carpet, the bottom of the sofa, the side of the coffee table, and the remote control that had fallen on the floor. She pounced on a tennis ball, and Larry sat on the floor and joined the game, rolling the ball across the floor. He loved the way she bounced as she ran and how her paws almost looked too big for her little legs. When Gracie tripped carrying the ball back to Larry, he scooped her up in his arms. "Don't worry, you'll grow into those paws."

After scarfing down her dinner and going out for the last walk of the night, Larry led Gracie into the master bedroom.

He set her in a large box with high sides he had placed next to his side of the bed. She would eventually sleep on her doggie bed in her crate, but while she adjusted to her new home, he wanted to keep her close and allow her to see him. Gracie sniffed the blankets on the bottom of the box, then curled into a ball in the corner.

When Larry turned off the light, Gracie started to whine and cry, and began scratching at the side of the box.

"You're okay, Gracie." Larry rubbed the puppy's head. She licked his fingers, then lay down beneath his hand. "I'm right here. I'm not going anywhere."

Gracie must have believed him because she fell fast asleep.

❧

Gracie's first few weeks were filled with lots of playtime, numerous short walks around the town house complex where they met and interacted with their neighbors, quiet mornings lying at Larry's feet while he read his Bible, and visits from family and friends. Brooke brought Luke to meet the puppy, but they all decided to wait a few more weeks before Gracie was introduced to Cody. Larry was sure the two would get along well, but he wanted Gracie to settle in and get comfortable with him before putting her in a situation that might frighten her. He wanted her to trust him. Since she was running to him whenever she heard an unfamiliar sound, he was confident that he was becoming her safe place.

Every moment that Larry wasn't with Cody, he was with Gracie. "I promise, you'll meet Cody soon," he told her one day after he got back from visiting Charlie and Shelba. It had been a wonderful but draining day. Gracie ran up to him, wagging her tail and sniffing his pant legs and shoes. When she let out a high-pitched bark, Larry knew it was time to take Gracie to Brooke's house.

❧

"Easy girl," Larry corrected, pulling back gently on the puppy's leash to get her to walk beside him. "Side."

In the month since Gracie had arrived, she'd already mastered Sit and Stay, was getting close to mastering Down and Wait, and had only had one accident in the house. She was eager to learn and quick to understand. And she continually impressed Larry with her calm demeanor and go-with-the-flow personality.

"You are going to make a wonderful therapy dog," he said as he rang Brooke's doorbell.

Cody's deep, throaty bark startled Gracie, who backed up and hid behind Larry's legs.

"Cody's a big dog, but he's going to be your best buddy," Larry reassured her.

Gracie let out an unconvinced whimper.

When Brooke opened the front door, Cody rushed to Larry. But just before he reached Larry's side, he spotted Gracie. Her tail remained firmly between her legs while Cody sniffed her head. Cody glanced at Larry, then resumed his investigation, sniffing Gracie's legs, paws, and back end. He then lowered his chest into an eager play-bow. Gracie, sensing that the bigger dog meant her no harm, bounded over to Cody and nosed his ears.

The two dogs ran in circles and play-wrestled with each other in the fenced backyard until their tongues were hanging from their mouths and they needed to come in for water. Cody graciously shared his water bowl with Gracie, and in minutes the two had emptied it. The new friends sprawled on the tile floor for a quick recharge, then were let outside again to end a very good day.

"I'll be back tomorrow, Cody," Larry said. "We need to go see Charlie."

Charlie's condition had been deteriorating over the past few weeks, and he admitted to Larry that he was ready to go home to heaven. His only hesitation was that he didn't want to leave Shelba.

"I love that woman more than my own life," he had told Larry the day he officiated a renewal of their wedding vows. The simple ceremony took place in Charlie's hospital room, with their daughters and Larry, Susan, and Cody as witnesses, as well as several of Charlie's favorite nurses and doctors.

Larry had been honored to lead the bittersweet service but also was grateful to return home and be greeted by Gracie. The puppy's exuberance and energy helped ease the pain of watching Charlie slowly slip away.

The puppy slept soundly in the back seat on the drive home from Brooke's.

"I think she and Cody are going to be good friends," Susan said.

"I knew they would be. And they need to be, because Cody is going to help me teach her how to be a therapy dog."

🐾

A week after meeting Cody, Gracie attended her first official puppy class at a nearby pet supplies store. Happily wagging her tail, she greeted each of the seven other puppies and their owners. She took a special interest in a hound named Bullet and a Golden Retriever named Bailey, but when the instructor said it was time to begin, Gracie left her new playmates and stood at Larry's side.

She was the star of the class, thanks to the training Larry had already started with her. The instructor even used Gracie to demonstrate a handful of commands.

"She's a natural," Bullet's owner, Sarah, commented, as the puppies engaged in free play during the last fifteen minutes of class.

"Thank you," Larry said, smiling proudly at Gracie. "I've been working with her a lot at home. She's going to be a therapy dog."

"Really? What made you decide to do that?"

"How much time do you have?" he said, chuckling. "The short answer is that I believe God told me to."

He half expected Sarah to excuse herself at that point, but she surprised him. "And the long answer?"

"God planted the seeds of this ministry in my heart long ago, when he brought a special Basset Hound named Gus into my life.

Gus helped me through a very difficult season by reminding me that God was still with me and would never leave me. Then two years ago, I felt God calling me to begin a therapy dog ministry. I started it with my wife, Susan, and her daughter's dog, Cody. Now we have more than twenty teams going to nursing homes, hospitals, care facilities, and schools to bring God's love to people through the beautiful dogs he's created—like Gracie.

"She was donated by a kind breeder who wanted her to be a part of this ministry. So we named her Grace, just like God's free grace to us. That's what Canines for Christ is all about—partnering with sweet dogs to extend the free gift of God's grace and love to others in our community."

When Gracie bounded over to him, Larry realized most of the other dogs and owners had left the enclosed area. "I warned you it was a long answer," he said sheepishly.

But Sarah smiled. "That was really inspiring. In fact, maybe Bullet and I can volunteer with you someday." As she bent down to attach the leash to his collar, the rambunctious hound enthusiastically licked her face. "That is, when he's a little older and more obedient."

"We would love to have you both."

"All right, Miss Gracie," Larry said, opening the rear door of his SUV. "Let's go to the mall and meet some people."

Larry had contacted the shopping center's corporate office two days earlier about taking his therapy-dog-in-training inside the mall. Since she wasn't a service dog, Larry needed to get permission to take her inside, and was delighted when permission was quickly granted.

Gracie certainly looked the part of a therapy dog. She was wearing a black therapy-dog-in-training vest, and Larry knew it wouldn't be long before she would be sporting one of the red vests with the ministry's new name—Canines for Christ—embroidered in gold lettering. Larry loved that the colors represented the gospel—the blood of Christ and the promise of heaven.

"You just be your sweet self, and I know God will work through you."

Gracie watched him carefully as he spoke. Larry wanted her to recognize the sound of his voice, his moods, his emotions, and his daily routine, all of which would help her become the therapy dog he knew she was meant to be.

Before they had taken four steps into Citrus Park Town Center, a young voice cried out, "A puppy!"

Immediately, Larry and Gracie were surrounded by a group of children and an exhausted-looking woman.

"Scoot back, guys." The woman attempted to wave the children back. "Sorry," she said apologetically to Larry.

"They're fine," Larry assured her, encouraging the children to come closer to Gracie.

Gracie's tail wagged double-time at all the attention. The youngsters giggled when Gracie lay on her back and started wiggling.

"Why did you bring a puppy in the mall?" one girl asked.

Larry smiled and asked Gracie to sit.

"Because this little puppy is learning to be a therapy dog," he said, rewarding Gracie with a pat and a training treat for obeying so quickly—especially with such enticing distractions surrounding her. "This is Gracie," he continued. "And she is going to help people know that they are loved."

"How's she gonna do that?" A young boy seemed skeptical.

"Well, did you see how excited she was to see you and how much she likes you?"

The boy nodded.

"Did you know that God likes you and loves you even more than that?"

The boy's eyes grew wider, and he shook his head.

"It's true. God loves you." Larry looked at each of the children and added, "He loves each of you." Then he looked at the woman, "He loves you too."

She averted her eyes, then looked at Gracie for a moment. She smiled politely, thanked Larry for his time, then told the children it was time to go eat lunch.

"Bye, Gracie!" a chorus of voices called out.

"I love you, too, Gracie!"

Larry didn't know which child had said those parting words, but it warmed his heart.

"You see? You already have a fan club, Gracie. And you planted a seed of hope. And we've only gone four steps!"

Larry walked Gracie up and down the main concourse, stopping whenever someone wanted to pet her or asked what the two of them were doing. Gracie met an elderly couple, a group of high-school students, a middle-aged woman, and a young family with two infants in tow. Larry marveled at how well she interacted with all of them. She wasn't afraid, and she only tried to jump up twice, quickly returning to Larry's side when he corrected her.

After walking through the food court—where every head seemed to turn—they stopped in front of the elevator.

"How about one last challenge for the day?"

When the doors opened with a *ding*, Gracie took two steps back. Larry stepped into the elevator and held the open-door button. He wouldn't push his young dog to get on. If she was too afraid, he would try again another day. She had already accomplished so much that he considered the day a huge success. But since she was on a roll, he wanted to see how she would do with the elevator—something she would need to get used to for her work at the VA hospital. Gracie tilted her head to the side as she observed Larry inside the elevator.

"It's okay. Come on, girl," he said encouragingly.

She backed up slightly, then bounded forward. Her tail swung with pride.

"What a brave and wonderful girl you are!"

Larry pushed the arrow to go up one floor. Gracie's legs tensed as the elevator moved and she kept her eyes locked on Larry.

"You're doing a great job, Gracie. We're almost there. This is a much easier way to get around than taking all those stairs. We're almost . . ."

Ding.

"There," he said as the doors opened. Larry led Gracie out of the elevator, and she did a body-wiggling shake, then looked up as if to say, "What's next?"

"Well, you might be willing to spend another hour here, but I'm tired. Let's go home."

He pushed the elevator button, and Gracie went right in and sat down like an elevator-riding pro.

🐾

Two weeks later, Larry was reading his Bible when the phone rang.

"Larry, it's Shelba." He could hear the pain in her voice. "Charlie is . . ." Her voice caught on a sob. "He's slipping away. Can you please bring Cody and sit with us for a while?"

Larry assured her that he and Cody would be there as quickly as possible.

After hanging up, Larry took a moment to pray. As he did, Gracie padded over and pawed at his leg. Even though she was nearly thirty pounds now, he still picked her up and held her on his lap.

"Father, thank you for Charlie and for Shelba, and for the time we've had with him. I wanted so badly for him to be healed on this earth, but I know he will soon experience a healing and joy that we can't even imagine." Gracie licked Larry's cheek, and her warm puppy-breath on his neck made him smile. "And thank you for this bundle of grace you've given us. Help Susan and me to offer comfort and support to Charlie and Shelba today."

An hour later, Larry, Susan, and Cody walked into Charlie's room in the intensive care unit. Larry's heart sank. Charlie had looked weak and frail when he'd seen him a few weeks ago, but now he looked like a shell of himself.

Susan held Shelba as Larry studied Charlie's face as he slept. It was sunken and had a grayish hue, but thanks to the morphine drip for pain, his expression was almost peaceful.

"The doctors say he should only last another day or two. He's off all food, and they are just keeping him comfortable. If only they could do that for me," Shelba said, wiping tears from her cheeks.

Cody walked to Shelba and nudged his head under her hand. That was all the invitation she needed. Shelba dropped to her knees and held on to the dog while she wept for her husband. Larry and Susan each put a hand on her shoulder. No words were spoken for several minutes. As Shelba's sobs stilled and she stood up, Cody walked to Charlie's bedside and looked up at Larry. The dog had spent many hours lying next to Charlie over the past several months. Larry hesitated, unsure what to do now.

"Please," Shelba nodded, "let him say goodbye."

Larry lifted Cody and gently laid him beside Charlie. Cody looked at Charlie, nudged his hand, then put his head on the dying man's chest.

"Charlie sure loves you, Cody," Shelba said. "You kept him company and were a good friend to him." Her voice broke on the last few words, but she still smiled gratefully.

Larry put one hand over Charlie's and the other on Cody's head and prayed for his friend—for what he knew would be the last time. Shelba had already asked Larry to lead Charlie's memorial service, but right now, his focus was on saying goodbye.

Charlie and Shelba's daughters arrived twenty minutes later. After Larry and Susan greeted them, the two women gravitated to Cody and began hugging and petting him. After a while, Larry and Susan knew it was time to leave the family alone to grieve so they gave Shelba and her daughters a final round of hugs and said they'd be in touch. It was a quiet ride home, the weight of grief too heavy for words and too sacred to attempt a conversation.

After dropping Cody off and arriving home, Larry took Gracie for a short walk. The four-month-old puppy's excitement over a simple outing helped lift Larry's spirits. *From the sorrow of death to the joy of life, you remain the same, Father*, he prayed.

Gracie followed her nose, zigzagging down the sidewalk, stopping to pounce on an oak leaf before chasing a butterfly.

"You are like medicine for a weary soul, Gracie."

As the pair rounded a bend, a little girl riding a pink and purple tricycle zoomed in front of her mother and made a beeline for Gracie.

"Ask first!" her mother called out.

"Can I pet your dog?" the child asked, leaving her tricycle in the middle of the sidewalk as she ran straight for Gracie.

Pink barrettes dangled from the ends of her hair, and Larry wondered how Gracie would react to them. Would they look like a toy? Would she try to grab them? He was prepared to intervene should the puppy give any indication of wanting to play with the bright objects.

But when he asked Gracie to sit and invited the little girl over, he realized he needn't have worried. The puppy simply sniffed the girl's feet, licked her hands, and rolled over for a belly rub.

"Your dog is so cute," she said, laughing as Gracie began to chew a dried leaf.

Larry learned that her name was Sasha, her mom's name was Val, and they had recently moved into the complex. He gathered that Sasha had yet to make any friends, and so when she asked if she could visit Gracie again soon, he didn't hesitate.

"Gracie loves meeting new friends, and by the way she's wagging her tail and following you, I can tell she really likes you."

"I like you too," Sasha said, getting her face close enough to Gracie for the puppy to lick her cheek.

After saying goodbye to Sasha and Val and greeting several more neighbors, Larry and Gracie made their way back home. Larry's heart and mind were full, yet the pain of loss quickly settled back over him. But when Gracie tripped over her own feet while zooming around the family room, he couldn't help but laugh. He knew the grief over Charlie's passing would be with him for a while. But for the moment, a joyful pup was trying to climb up his shirt and plant kisses on his chin.

CHAPTER TEN

SEVERAL MONTHS AFTER OFFICIATING Charlie's memorial service, Larry led Gracie down the paint aisle of Home Depot to pick up the color Susan had requested for their guest bath. As he passed the brush and roller display, a young boy wearing Spider-Man pajamas called out, "I like your dog!" Gracie's tail waved a happy greeting as the boy approached. "Can I say hi? My dad said it was okay."

A man balancing a stack of light bulbs in one arm and a wiggling toddler in the other nodded at Larry.

"Just a quick hi," the frazzled father called out as the toddler lurched for the top box of bulbs.

Eight-month-old Gracie sniffed the boy's blue Crocs as he ran his fingers through Gracie's fur.

"Why did you bring a dog to Home Depot?" he laughed.

"Because I'm teaching her to be a special kind of dog called a therapy dog. They have to be comfortable in all kinds of places with all kinds of noises. So I bring Gracie with me everywhere I can. And today I needed to get some paint so I brought her here."

"So you're like her teacher?"

"I guess I *am* like her teacher."

"My teacher's name is Mrs. Allen, but she doesn't let us go to Home Depot. She just teaches us math and stuff."

Larry chuckled at the talkative boy, then his frazzled father told him it was time to go.

"Bye, Gracie. Hope you have fun at Home Depot school!" he said, darting away.

Gracie eagerly looked at Larry with her bright eyes as if to ask, "What's next?"

"You are a great student, Gracie," Larry praised. "And a really good friend too." He reached into his pocket and pulled out the paint color sample Susan had given him and placed a gallon of white flat paint on the counter to have the colors added. He and Susan had decided to move to a new development being built in Lutz and rent out their current town house. Their new house wouldn't be ready for several months, so Susan thought they should repaint and make some minor repairs on the town house before potential renters saw it. As Larry waited for the paint to finish mixing, he leaned over to Gracie. "Now, if only I could teach you how to paint."

🐾

A week later, after repainting almost every room in their town house, Larry and Susan took Cody and Gracie to the Trinity school. Cody had been to the arts-focused facility for adults with mental and developmental challenges every week for the past nine months, and now it was Gracie's turn. The white Lab's excitement was evident as she leapt from the car and zigzagged back and forth with her nose to the ground, trying to take in every new smell. Susan opened the passenger side rear door for eight-year-old Cody. He jumped from the car, shook from nose to tail, visited the grassy area, and then sat awaiting Larry's command.

Larry had been looking forward to this day—Gracie's first official Canines for Christ visit—since the first day he met her. Granted, it was a training visit for the puppy who wouldn't formally take over for Cody until after her first birthday. But she was ready to start learning the ropes from Cody. Gracie was wearing her red Canines for Christ vest instead of her black training one. She would be following Cody's lead.

With the ministry expanding to thirty teams, Larry had witnessed firsthand how helpful it was to have a new dog learn from a veteran dog. And since Cody was the most experienced therapy dog in the ministry, he was often cast in the role of lead dog when a new volunteer team joined. Once a dog was certified through the Canine Good Citizen test, Larry would meet with the dog and the volunteer, and if both parties agreed the ministry was a good fit, they initially would accompany Larry and Cody. Those visits gave the volunteers hands-on practice and allowed Larry to observe a new dog in action, but they also helped build relationships between new volunteers and employees at the sites they visited. It was a model that worked well for them. And deep down, Larry loved that most of the dogs in the ministry had been trained by Cody.

"You're a good teacher." Dependable, loving, happy-go-lucky Cody. A borrowed dog who turned out to be God's gracious provision for a ministry he hadn't gone looking for. A sweet memory of Gus came to mind, and Larry once again marveled at how God had planted the seeds for Canines for Christ all those years ago through

Gus. He had watered and nourished them through Cody. And now, he was preparing Gracie to take the lead. *All this time, God has been leading me to this work. To this moment, this ministry. To his Grace.*

"Well, Cody and Gracie," he said, looking from one dog to the other, "are you ready to go to work?"

Cody sprang up. Gracie jumped up a fraction of a second later and studied the older dog as if trying to understand what had caused Cody's reaction.

"It's time to go to work, Gracie," Larry repeated, knowing it wouldn't take long for his smart puppy to connect the phrase with making visits. After all, it had only taken Cody a few weeks to understand that *go to work* meant lots of attention, new friends, and fun. In fact, the words made Cody so excited that Larry had to be careful not to use the phrase unless they were going to make an official visit.

He had learned that lesson last year when he and Susan were at Brooke's house, helping with a landscaping project. When Larry announced it was time to go to work on the mulch pile, Cody was so ecstatic that they had to go to a nearby nursing home for a short visit with some of the residents so he would calm down.

Larry and Susan led the two dogs through the glass doors of the Trinity school building. As Larry signed them in, Cody and Gracie received attention from the receptionist and from Terry Cone, the woman who had initially contacted Larry about bringing therapy dogs to their facility.

Terry was the programs coordinator at Trinity and also a volunteer at the VA hospital. After hearing about the positive impact Cody and Larry were having there, Terry had called him about visiting Trinity. So far, the experience had greatly exceeded any expectations Larry may have had.

He fondly recalled the first time he had entered the school nine months earlier. A baby grand piano was in the center of the lobby, being played by a middle-aged man. Larry assumed he was a hired professional pianist.

"That's Lloyd, a student here," Terry had explained. "It took a while for him to engage in any of our programs, but one day he pointed to the piano, and we encouraged him to sit on the bench. We were all blown away when he started to play." Larry could understand why. Lloyd's talent was remarkable.

"His autism makes it hard for him to connect with people, but when he plays it's like he reaches through the keys and touches all of our hearts."

Larry was tempted to say something to Lloyd but he didn't want to interrupt the beautiful music pouring out of the man's heart and mind, not written down on paper. Instead, he simply waved at Lloyd as he followed Terry.

"This building used to be a nursing home. The layout is perfect for us—two wings for our higher functioning students, with a lunchroom, a large multipurpose room, and several smaller classrooms. The third wing is reserved for students with more significant behavioral issues and needs, and the fourth wing is for our students who need the most specialized attention and care."

Larry admired the cheerful paintings; the clean tile floors; the bright, warm lighting; and the pleasant smell.

"This really is a beautiful and welcoming facility."

"Dog!" A male voice shouted from an open door on the right side of the hallway.

Terry chuckled and motioned Larry into the room. The bags of crackers and water bottles on the tables in the room were evidence it was snack time.

"We don't mean to interrupt," Terry said to the three staff members standing near the front of the room. "I was just giving Larry and his dog, Cody, a tour. They are going to start coming here to visit with all of us. What do you guys think about that?"

A chorus of cheers and shouts of "Yes!" rang out.

Larry led Cody around the room, stopping at each person who showed the slightest interest in him.

"Cody and I are so glad to meet you," Larry said to each person, looking them in the eye and, in some cases, squeezing a shoulder or shaking a hand.

Terry had mentioned that some of the challenges their students faced included autism, cerebral palsy, Down syndrome, birth defects, cognitive impairment, spina bifida, and traumatic brain injuries, but in that moment, all Larry could see were excited faces, eager to make a new friend. And for his part, Cody was thrilled to be that new friend. The Golden sat for pats to his head and back, lay down beside those who were sitting on the floor, and put his paws up on the wheelchair lapboards of those who couldn't bend down to touch him. His wagging tail and drooping tongue were big hits among the students, whose ages ranged from twenty-two to seventy-nine.

After leaving the first classroom, Larry and Cody followed Terry to ten others. Several were similar to the first, with a few others containing less ambulatory students. Cody didn't hesitate when Larry repeated the Paws Up command over and over. In the two classrooms with the most severely impacted students, who didn't seem to react to any stimuli, Larry led Cody to each one and either placed his hand on the student's shoulder or placed their hand on Cody's back. Terry told Larry each person's name so he could greet them personally. Larry had no way of knowing if the students were aware of his and Cody's presence, but he knew God was aware of them. He and Cody would share God's love as best they could.

It had been a beautiful and exhausting day. As Larry had followed Terry back toward the main lobby, he knew Trinity would become an important part of the Canines for Christ ministry. That feeling was confirmed when a man named Ed hurried from his classroom, waving his arms and making excited sounds. A woman wearing a Trinity shirt hurried after him.

"Ed would like to say goodbye to Cody," the woman explained. "He was feeling a little nervous when you first came in, but I think he's feeling better now and wants to say hi, if that's okay."

"That is most definitely okay," Larry said, extending his hand toward Ed.

Larry guessed Ed was in his late forties or early fifties as he watched him drop to the floor in the main hallway and pat his lap. Cody didn't hesitate. He stretched out against Ed's leg and laid his head on the man's lap. Ed beamed at Larry, then began talking to Cody with guttural sounds that no one but God, and perhaps Cody, could understand. Ed ran his arm back and forth over Cody's back and smiled so wide Larry wondered if his cheeks would be sore later. Cody ran his tongue over the back of his new friend's hand, eliciting a laugh from Ed so infectious that everyone standing near him began to laugh.

"What a gift you gave Ed," Larry said to Cody after their visit. "What a gift you gave all of us."

Now, as Gracie followed Cody down the same hallway where they had first met Ed, Larry wondered how she would do with the Trinity students. He had exposed her to a wide variety of people in all kinds of settings. But he wondered how she would handle the sounds, range of excitement, and special needs she would experience up and down Trinity's hallways. How would she react to a wheelchair? How would she handle so many hands reaching for her at the same time? How would she respond to Ed's childlike exuberance? Larry instinctively tightened his grip on Gracie's leash. *Father, please let her follow Cody's lead. Work through Gracie and Cody to bring your love and presence to each person we meet.*

Larry had barely finished his silent prayer when he heard Ed's squeal of delight. He was smiling broadly and waving his arms. He walked to Cody, dropped to the floor, and patted his lap. Cody leaned his head against Ed's chest for a moment, then sprawled himself across the man's lap. Ed buried his head in Cody's fur and made a series of sounds. After several minutes, he raised his head and gestured wildly toward Gracie. She took two tentative steps forward, then stopped and looked at Larry.

"Go on," Larry encouraged. "Say hi to Ed."

Gracie was excited as she neared Ed and Cody. Ed kept one hand on Cody and extended the other to Gracie.

"Ed, this is our dog Gracie," Larry explained. "She is going to start making visits with us. Cody is her teacher and he's helping her learn how to be a therapy dog. They both are so happy to see you."

Ed looked at his teacher before focusing on the two dogs. His smile widened and he made a loud screeching sound. Larry held his breath. Would Gracie be scared and run away? Gracie bounded toward Ed, close enough to run her tongue over his ruddy cheek, which made him squeal in delight even more. Then she nuzzled beside Cody and laid her head on Ed's lap.

"Two dogs!" A woman was standing in the doorway of the classroom across the hall. "Two dogs are out here!"

Terry assured her the dogs would come to her room next. When Terry told Ed it was time for Cody and Gracie to meet the other students, he kissed each dog's head. However, instead of remaining in his classroom, he followed the dogs into the next classroom, and the next. Ed stayed with Cody and Gracie the entire time they were at Trinity.

"I guess Ed's decided to serve as your escort," Terry chuckled, as they entered the large multipurpose room.

Men and women were sitting at tables covered in art supplies. Some were painting with brushes, others were using their fingers. Some were working with clay, while others held glue sticks. The atmosphere was charged with the excitement of creating art. But it became supercharged when Cody and Gracie entered the room.

"It's Cody the Wonder Dog!"

In an instant everyone was gathered around Cody.

"Cody has a sidekick," a man named Earl announced. All eyes turned to Gracie, and her tail began wagging in circles. Ed smiled like a proud father.

Larry introduced Gracie to the group, much the same way he had introduced her to Ed.

"Hi, Gracie," Earl said, holding out his hand.

Larry's heart swelled as his puppy placed her paw in Earl's open hand.

"Um, uh, Mr. Larry?" A woman named Leslie was tugging on Larry's sleeve. "Marianne is in the hospital. She sits beside me in art class. But she's not here. I miss her." Leslie's blue eyes filled with tears.

"I am so sorry to hear that, Leslie," Larry said, putting his arm around her. "It's hard when our friends get sick and can't be with us."

Leslie laid her head on Larry's shoulder. "Will you say a prayer for Marianne? My mama used to pray for me when I was in the hospital."

"Of course I will. Thank you for asking me. God loves it when we pray for each other."

Larry kept his arm around Leslie as he prayed. He asked God to heal Marianne, and to help her feel his love and peace while she was in the hospital. He also prayed for peace and comfort for Leslie and all of Marianne's friends and family. After saying amen, he opened his eyes and was surprised to find most of the class standing around him. Many of them had bowed their heads, and several mumbled amen.

"My . . . my . . . um, my cousin has to have sir . . . sir-cha-ry," a young man in a wheelchair said.

"My kitty-cat is sick," a woman added, wiping her cheeks.

"I have to go to the doctor tomorrow." Earl shuddered at the thought. "I don't like the doctor."

After several other students called out their concerns, Larry asked if he could pray for each one of them. They all nodded, and Larry bowed his head again. He prayed for each student by name, and when he paused or stumbled, Earl or Terry quickly supplied the person's name and concern. Larry finished by thanking God for how much he loved each and every person at Trinity and praising him for how special they all were. This time when Larry said amen, everyone shouted, "AMEN!"

As Larry and Susan drove to Cody's house, they discussed adding a few more teams to the Trinity rotation, and decided that each weekly visit should end with a time for prayer requests. Larry loved praying with every person they interacted with, but there was something extra special about the prayer time at Trinity. Something sacred and powerful about praying with people who often feel unseen or unheard—people who are often dismissed because of their differences. Today, as they'd stood together in the presence of a sovereign, loving God, it had felt as if heaven bent toward earth and God whispered, *I see you. You are loved.*

And Larry knew God was showing his love and presence through the dogs' wet kisses and wagging tails.

After dropping Cody off, Larry and Susan took Gracie by their new house, just a foundation and framed walls right now. Progress was slow but steady, and each time they came by, Larry became more enthused about the move. Theirs was one of the first houses being built in the new development. The cleared lots were surrounded by untouched wilderness, small lakes, and nature preserves. In the months they'd been visiting their new property, they had seen snakes, alligators, raccoons, and a coyote. They enjoyed glimpsing the wildlife, but also realized they needed to take precautions when walking Gracie. After spotting the coyote, Larry began carrying a large walking stick to protect Gracie when the two of them were out.

As they walked around their property, Larry and Susan thanked the men working on their home. They learned each of their names and introduced each one to Gracie. One man named Jorge wadded up some rags into a ball and threw it for Gracie, then play-wrestled her when she brought it back. *Leave it to Gracie to make friends everywhere she goes.*

CHAPTER ELEVEN

A WEEK AFTER THEIR VISIT TO TRINITY, Larry took Gracie into Walgreens with him to pick up a prescription. Now nine months old, Gracie still looked more puppy than adult, but her calm demeanor, thorough training, and official therapy dog status allowed Larry to take her places most other dog owners couldn't. Larry had received permission more than a year ago to bring Cody into Walgreens and since then had only entered the store once without a dog beside him. The drugstore proved to be a good place to interact with people who, unbeknownst to themselves, needed a visit with a therapy dog. That's what happened when they were leaving the store at the same time a woman was about to come in.

The first thing Larry noticed was the black back brace wrapped around her petite frame. She walked carefully, with hesitant and measured steps. Her teeth pressed into her bottom lip. It was clear the woman was in pain. Her slumping shoulders and faraway look made Larry suspect her pain was more than physical, something much deeper. Yet, the moment her eyes found Gracie, her entire face transformed into what Larry could only describe as bewildered hope.

"Oh, what a beautiful dog!" she gushed, heading straight for the white Lab.

Gracie turned toward the woman and sat without any prompt from Larry. He was proud of his young dog's instincts.

"I'm Larry and this is my dog, Gracie."

"I'm Laura," the woman said, bending her knees to better reach the dog. "I have a yellow Lab at home—Chloe. You remind me of her. Yes, you do, Gracie. She's still a puppy, right?"

"She's nine months old, and she's being trained to be a therapy dog."

Laura read Gracie's vest.

"Canines for Christ. So you're with a Christian therapy dog group?

"Yes, bringing God's loving-kindness to people," Larry answered. "We started off visiting nursing homes and the hospital, but now we have teams all over Tampa bringing hope and comfort to hospice patients, students, cancer patients . . ."

"And strangers outside of Walgreens," Laura interrupted with a chuckle.

"And to new friends everywhere," Larry reframed.

Laura closed her eyes briefly as she ran her fingers over Gracie's velvet-soft ears. Larry could sense that Laura had a story to tell him, but it was a story she wasn't quite ready to share. Instead, she told him that she had been looking for a place to volunteer.

"I'd love to help others in some way—which I think will also help me," she added. "I'd love to hear more about your ministry, and maybe even introduce you to my husband to see if this is something we could do together."

Larry detected a mix of hope and trepidation in her request and sought to ease any fears.

"I would love to meet with you and . . ." he hesitated, hoping she would supply her husband's name.

"Carl."

"I would love to meet with you, Carl, and Chloe. Getting to know prospective volunteers is one of my favorite parts of this ministry. Once you talk to Carl, give me a call, and we can set up a time to meet."

He handed her one of the Canines for Christ cards he carried with him at all times. The card had a photo of himself with Cody and Gracie, listed his contact information and the ministry's website, and included the words of John 3:16. Laura tucked the card in her purse.

"I met a new volunteer the other day at the Panera down the street. If that's convenient for you, we could meet there—whenever you are ready."

"You'll be hearing from me soon," Laura assured him.

🐾

Another week passed and Larry awoke earlier than usual. His ankle was hurting and he tried to stretch, but he was afraid his movements would awaken Susan, so he quietly climbed out of bed. The day's itinerary was full of visits before an afternoon appointment with Laura and Carl. He might as well get a head start on the day. Gracie followed him out of the room.

"It's still a little early for you to eat," Larry said, rubbing the sleepy dog's head. "How about we spend some time with God first and then I'll get you breakfast?"

Seemingly satisfied with the plan, Gracie followed Larry over to his recliner. He reached for his Bible and glanced at Gracie, who had curled up at his feet.

"Lord, this is how I want to live my life—at your feet. Waiting for you, trusting you, near you. Please keep my heart as close to you as Gracie is close to me. Thank you for this beautiful dog. Bless her, Lord. And work through both of us to show your love to others."

The next thirty minutes Larry talked and listened to God, while Gracie slept peacefully at his feet.

That afternoon, Larry and Gracie found an outdoor table at Panera to wait for Laura, Carl, and Chloe. The day after Larry and Laura met, she had called to schedule their prospective volunteer appointment.

"Gracie, sit," Larry instructed, as a server placed a plate of muffins and three coffees on the table.

Larry wasn't sure if they drank coffee, but he wanted to offer them a mid-afternoon snack during their meeting.

"Your dog is so sweet," the server said. "Can I pet her?"

Larry smiled warmly and introduced Gracie. The young server, whose name tag read "Zara," knelt in front of the dog and rubbed the thick fur on her chest.

"We always had dogs when I was growing up, but now I live in a small apartment and I can't have one."

"Well, I pray that one day you will get your very own dog, and in the meantime, every time I bring Gracie here, we will be sure to find you and say hi."

Moments later, Larry spotted Laura with a man holding a leash with a yellow Lab at the end. The man seemed a bit hesitant, but Laura tugged on his arm, and coaxed the two forward.

Larry waved them over.

"Gracie and I went ahead and got a table," he said, as Laura gave him a hug.

"This is Carl, and this is our Chloe." Laura looked at them lovingly.

Larry shook Carl's hand, then greeted Chloe. However, Chloe was far more interested in Gracie. The two Labs sniffed each other thoroughly, then put their heads together.

"It looks like the girls are swapping secrets," Larry joked. After giving the new canine friends time to get to know each other, Larry asked Gracie to sit, while he knelt in front of Chloe.

"Well, hello there, Miss Chloe," he said, running his hands down her back and up her sides. "It is very nice to meet you. I hear you have been very helpful to Laura."

Chloe leaned her head against Larry. He could tell she was a gentle and calm dog—and would likely be a perfect addition to the ministry. He motioned for Laura and Carl to sit across from him and enjoy the muffins and coffee. Carl took a muffin and a coffee, but Laura seemed too excited to eat. Chloe turned her attention from Gracie to the muffin in Carl's hand. He mumbled for her to sit.

"Thank you both for meeting with me today," Larry began. "And thank you for bringing Chloe. She is a beautiful dog and very well-behaved." His words made the couple smile proudly at her.

"Laura, when I first met you, I sensed you had a story to share with me. Would you mind telling me a little bit about yourself and why you want to volunteer with Canines for Christ?"

Laura pressed her lips together in a half-smile and nodded.

"Sure," she answered, with a quick glance to Carl, who placed his hand on her arm. "Two years ago, as I was driving back to my office after a meeting, I was hit by an eighteen-year-old drunk driver going 50 mph in a 35 mph zone. I don't remember anything about the crash. I was told that an off-duty fireman heard the impact and rushed to the scene. He actually thought I was dead, but after finding a faint pulse, he cleared my airway and revived me." Laura trembled slightly, and Carl patted her hand. "Soon after that, EMS arrived on the scene and the paramedics had to use the Jaws of Life to free me from my mangled car. I was airlifted to the hospital, where I was given a 2 percent chance of survival."

Larry couldn't imagine the trauma of such an unexpected horrific accident or the agony her family and friends must have endured as they waited for word of her status.

"You are a walking miracle," he observed.

"I really believe I am," she agreed. "I had to spend six weeks in a drug-induced coma for the bleeding in my brain to stop so the doctors could repair my aorta." She paused and then looked at the dogs as she continued her story.

"When I was in the coma, I . . ." she paused and took a deep breath, "I believe God spoke to me and said, 'This is not your time. I have more for you to do.' I know that might sound crazy to some people . . ."

"It doesn't sound crazy to me," Larry reassured her.

Laura smiled in relief. "Thank you. I really do believe he said that to me. I mean I shouldn't be here. They showed me pictures of what was left of my car, which were really hard to see. None of the first responders expected me to survive—but I did. And even though my injuries and the severe head trauma have left me permanently disabled—and I still struggle with anger and resentment toward the driver—I can't deny that my life is a gift." She squeezed Carl's hand. "And it's a gift I want to dedicate to God." She looked at Chloe and Gracie. "I've always loved dogs. In fact, the sweet dog we had at the time of my accident became my self-appointed protector during my recovery. I was so upset when he passed away that we went right to a shelter and adopted Chloe. She and I have formed a strong bond since I spend a lot of time at home because I can't work."

She paused for another moment. She chewed her bottom lip then leaned forward.

"I had been a successful events manager at a country club, and having to leave my job coupled with the constant pain I'm in has done a number on my mental health and self-worth. I love spending time with Carl and Chloe, but some days can get hard—really hard and really dark."

She took a long, slow breath. As she did, Chloe stood and walked to her with Gracie following behind. They stood in front of Laura who rested a hand on each dog. It was as if they were offering her their strength.

"Sometimes the only thing that helps me endure is remembering what God whispered to me when I was in the coma. And so I've been asking him to help me find a purpose for my new life—a way to honor him and make a difference for others. And then, I meet you and Gracie and learn about Canines for Christ! I really feel that this is what I'm supposed to be doing. Maybe this is part of why God saved me?" She spoke the last few words as if a question to herself.

Larry leaned back in his chair. Laura had been near death two years ago, around the very same time God was laying the idea for a therapy dog ministry on his heart. And now she was asking how to become a volunteer. *Only you, Lord,* Larry marveled.

"What a tragic and yet amazing story of God's provision and purpose over your life. And how wonderful that you want to work with your beautiful dog to share his love and hope with others— especially those who have been through similar experiences. God has a purpose and a plan for your life, and I would love to think that Canines for Christ might play a role in helping you find that purpose. Can I ask an important question though?"

Laura nodded.

"As much as I would love to have you join us, I don't want you to put your own health or recovery at risk. Do you feel like you are well enough to visit people in hospitals, nursing homes, special-needs facilities, and other places?"

Laura leaned forward and placed her elbows on the table.

"I'm sure there will be days that I don't feel well enough to visit those places, but I'm getting pretty good at knowing my limits. I'm also getting tired of letting my limits define me. So if you're willing to have me—to have us," she glanced hopefully at Carl, "then I'd love the chance to see if it works."

Larry smiled and nodded.

"How does all of this sound to you, Carl?"

"I just want what I've always wanted—to see that sparkle in her eyes again." Carl's eyebrows furrowed with a memory. "She was so broken," he said. "When I walked into that hospital room, I didn't think . . ." he cleared his throat. "I didn't know if I would ever get to see that sparkle again. But there it is," he pointed at Laura. "And that's all that matters. So even though I've never done anything like this before, and we don't really know what all we'll be doing, I'm willing to find out. And we'll make it work."

After talking more about Laura's recovery, hearing the account of her accident from Carl's perspective, and sharing some of his own story with Larry, the three of them decided that after getting Chloe certified through the Canine Good Citizen test, Laura would bring her on a joint visit with Larry and either Cody or Gracie. Larry hoped that the joint visits would help her become more comfortable with the process and allow her to see how dogs can bring God's love and comfort to people.

Larry knew it would likely be a difficult road for Laura. It was obvious she was still in pain—both physically and emotionally. And he suspected seeing some of the patients in a hospital setting was going to be hard for her. But he and Susan would make themselves available as mentors and prayer partners. And if Larry's instincts were right, Laura—and likely Carl too—would become an important part of the ministry.

CHAPTER TWELVE

AFTER LEAVING PANERA, Larry picked up Cody and Susan for their weekly visit to Suncoast Kids Place.

When they entered the bright, cheerful lobby, Cody sat calmly for the children. The Golden Retriever knew the routine well. But since this was Gracie's first time in the building, she was eager to explore. Wanting her to feel comfortable in the unfamiliar space, Larry left Cody with Susan and let Gracie lead the way for him. Her inquisitive search brought back sweet memories of Cody's first visit to Sister Agnes. Gracie's nose stayed pressed toward the floor as she investigated the playroom filled with books, puzzles, and toys. Larry chuckled when Gracie play-bowed in front of an inflatable ball but told her to leave it. As much as he wanted to indulge her love of play, she needed to learn that when she was wearing her vest, she was working. There would be plenty of time to play after their visits. As they were returning to the lobby, Gracie heard children's voices.

"Cody!"

Gracie charged forward.

"Easy girl," Larry corrected her, pleased when Gracie stopped and looked at him. "We approach new friends slowly."

Gracie slowed her pace to match Larry's as the pair rejoined Susan and Cody at the front doors. Four children surrounded the dogs, while their grandmother spoke quietly with the counselors. Each of the children greeted Cody first, then moved to Gracie—except one. Six-year-old Hayden kept his hand on Cody's back while his sister and two cousins were introduced to the newest member of the Canines for Christ family. Gracie's tail swung in a wide, happy arc as she greeted the three children. She kissed their outstretched hands, bounced on her front paws when two of the children showed her how high they could jump in their new shoes, and spun in circles when one of the little girls showed off her new dress with an impressive twirl. Larry and Susan exchanged a proud, but bewildered look. *Was Gracie mimicking the children?*

Larry shook off the question as he noticed Hayden's downcast expression. The boy's hand was still on Cody's back, and his bottom lip was pressed between his teeth.

"Hello there, Hayden," Larry said, switching leashes with Susan, so that he could stand closer to the boy. "I'm glad I get to see you today. And I know Cody's glad to see you again too." Hayden's slender fingers pushed deeper into Cody's thick red fur. "Cody is your friend, isn't he?"

Hayden nodded, his eyes not meeting Larry's. "Would you like to meet Cody's dog friend, Gracie? We brought her with us today because she's going to start making visits with us too. Just like Cody."

When Hayden cast a wary look at Gracie, Larry remembered the boy's grandmother telling him that just before her husband's death four months earlier, Hayden had been chased by a dog while playing outside with his cousins. Larry suspected Gracie might resemble the dog that had chased him.

"It's okay if you don't want to meet Gracie," Larry assured him. "She's a puppy, and she's still training to be a therapy dog. She needs to learn that sometimes people don't feel like a visit, and that sometimes they might even feel a little scared—and that's fine. So she can just watch you today. How does that sound?"

Hayden nodded up at Larry and whispered, "Okay."

The boy gave Gracie a slight wave as he ran to join his sister and cousins in the playroom.

"Gracie did wonderfully," Susan praised, as she and Larry traded back leashes and resumed their post by the door.

Cody and Gracie would be on hand if the four children in the playroom requested a dog join them in the session. But they were also there to greet a new child whose father had taken his own life just three weeks earlier. Larry's shoulders straightened as a young woman approached the front doors. She held a frightened-looking girl by the hand. Larry knew the mother's name was Emily, and her eight-year-old daughter's name was Ava. During her initial call, Emily had shared that Ava hadn't spoken much since losing her father.

Lord, please work through us. Please show your love and tenderness to this heartbroken mother and daughter. As Larry sent up a silent prayer for help, one of the grief counselors asked Susan if she would bring Cody into the counseling room. Hayden was asking for him. Larry nodded for her to go. He and Gracie would greet Emily and Ava.

Larry opened the glass doors and smiled warmly. "Hello. You must be Emily and Ava," he said, extending his hand. "I'm Chaplain Larry and this is my dog, Gracie."

Larry was still getting used to the title he had earned a few weeks earlier after completing the chaplain course. Emily attempted a weak smile and Ava ducked behind her mother.

"Gracie and I would also like to introduce you to Ms. Trish," he said, motioning to the grief counselor Ava would be working with.

Trish greeted Ava first and then Emily. She invited Ava into the playroom to see the different games and toys. While Ava worked on a puzzle, Trish spoke with Emily near the welcome desk. Larry knew the seasoned counselor wanted Emily to feel at ease so she was answering any questions Emily had about the counseling services her daughter would be receiving. He also knew Trish would provide an opportunity for the bereaved mother to share any details she didn't want to discuss in front of her daughter.

While Emily and Trish talked, Larry and Gracie slowly approached Ava.

"Hi, Ava," he said softly. "I'm guessing you like puzzles. I like them too. Do you like dogs?"

Ava kept her eyes on the puzzle but gave one quick nod.

"I really like dogs too, especially Gracie. She's very gentle and sweet. Would you like to say hi to her?"

Ava glanced quickly at her mom, who nodded her approval. Ava looked at Gracie and dipped her head slightly. Larry kept pressure on Gracie's leash, a wordless command to approach slowly. Gracie received the message. She eased herself beside the little girl and sat.

"Would you like to shake Gracie's hand?" Larry asked, kneeling down beside the girl.

Ava studied Gracie's face but didn't respond.

"I can't promise that she will do it, because she's still learning, but if you put your hand out like this," Larry stretched his arm toward his dog, "and say Paw, she will shake hands with you."

Gracie laid her paw in Larry's hand.

A hint of a smile flashed momentarily on Ava's face. She started to extend her hand, but then drew it back.

"If you'd like, you can put your hand out and I'll say *paw*. Do you want to try that?"

Ava nodded and reached toward Gracie.

"Gracie, say hello to Ava with your *paw*," he said, emphasizing the last word.

Gracie placed her paw gently on Ava's hand. When the little girl's fingers curled around Gracie's paw, Larry felt his throat constrict as he sat on the floor beside his dog.

"I can tell Gracie really likes you and feels safe with you."

A moment later, when Ava released Gracie's paw, the dog lay down and offered up her fuzzy belly for rubs. Ava's small fingers traced two large brown freckles in the middle of Gracie's belly. She then ran her hand up and down the dog's rib cage. When Gracie started wiggling on her back and making happy grunts, Ava smiled.

"It looks like Gracie made a new friend," Trish said, joining them on the floor.

Ava pulled her hand back to her side.

"Your mom told me that you like to draw," Trish said softly. "She's going to stay here and work on some boring grown-up paperwork. But I told her we have some art supplies down the hall, and she said she thought you might like that." Ava looked at her mom.

"Go ahead, baby," Emily encouraged, her voice hoarse.

"Would you like Gracie to come too?" Trish asked.

Ava twirled a section of blonde hair in her fingers and pulled it to her mouth as she nodded. While Larry kept hold of Gracie's leash, the dog walked in step with Ava into the counseling room. Ava was given her choice of markers, paints, or clay. She chose markers. Trish asked her to draw a picture of something that made her feel happy and she drew a picture of three people sitting around a dog—a small figure in a pink dress, a medium figure in a green dress, and a large figure in blue pants.

"Wow, you drew a beautiful picture of a dog," Trish praised. "My dogs always come out looking like camels."

Ava kept her eyes on her paper.

"Is that your dog in the picture?"

Ava shook her head and pointed to Gracie.

"I thought that might have been Miss Gracie. Is that your mom?" Ava nodded when Trish pointed to the figure in the green dress.

"Is that you?" Ava nodded again. She chewed her hair as she anticipated the counselor's next question.

"Is that your dad?" The little girl's brown eyes filled with tears as she nodded.

"Did he like dogs?" Trish asked gently.

As Ava nodded a second time, a tear spilled from her eye and landed on her paper—smearing the drawing of her dad. Ava wadded up the paper and pushed the markers away. Larry's heart broke for the child, who was experiencing a level of pain no one should have to endure, especially a child.

Gracie had been lying at Ava's feet and sat up at the sound of paper being crinkled. She looked first to Larry and then to her young friend. Gracie scooted closer to Ava's chair. When Ava forcefully pushed the markers away, Gracie laid her head on the child's lap. A small hand began stroking her head.

"Do you think your dad would like Gracie?" Trish's words were just above a whisper.

Ava's hair fell around her round face, hiding her eyes, as she rested her head against the back of Gracie's.

"Would you like to tell your dad about Gracie or draw him a picture of her?"

Ava sat up and looked at Trish. Her expression was confused, and if Larry wasn't mistaken, he detected a hint of anger.

"Sometimes when we're missing someone who has died, it can help us feel a little better if we talk to them, or write them a letter, or draw them a picture," Trish said to Ava. "Even though they aren't here anymore, we still have lots of big feelings and things we wish we could still tell them. Do you have things you wish you could tell your dad?"

Ava didn't move for several moments, but then she bobbed her head against Gracie.

"Well, I am going to put these markers and some paper right beside you, and you can decide if you want to use them."

Fifteen minutes later, Ava had drawn a picture of a dog on its back with heart freckles on its belly being rubbed by a stick figure of a smiling little girl, with blue tears dripping into a large puddle at her feet. A larger stick figure was standing behind the girl, dropping larger tears into the puddle. Ava drew several clouds and a black tornado at the top of the page, full of lightning bolts and raindrops. And she completed the picture with four colorful flowers, two trees, and a small, smiling sun in the upper right corner. She folded the picture and shoved it in her pocket.

She then took a second sheet of paper and drew the same dog

as before—complete with heart-shaped belly freckles, and with a happy looking girl standing beside her. When she finished, she handed the picture to Larry.

"Is this for me?" Larry asked, holding the picture reverently.

"Gracie," Ava whispered.

Gracie stood up at the sound of her name, the tip of her tail wagging in expectation.

"Gracie, look at this beautiful picture Ava made for you." Larry held the picture in front of his dog.

Gracie sniffed the paper from one corner to the other, then leaned her head around the drawing to kiss her friend's hand. An hour after they first met, Gracie escorted Ava back to the playroom where Hayden and the others were playing with Cody. Gracie stayed close to Ava, but happily interacted with Hayden's sister and cousins when they immediately ran over to say hi. Everyone came but Hayden. When Hayden's sister called him over, Gracie stopped wiggling and sat down. Larry was astonished at Gracie's sudden change in behavior—from excited to calm.

Hayden hesitated once he got within a foot of Gracie.

"She's nice," a soft voice said.

It was Ava.

The young girl put her arm around Gracie's back and motioned for Hayden to pet her. As the boy's small hand touched Gracie's side, Larry released the breath he didn't realize he had been holding. How was it possible to experience such joy in the midst of crushing grief? How could hurting children offer hope to each other—and to a room full of adults?

As Larry watched Hayden and Ava hug Gracie, he realized the answer had never been more obvious.

It was because of God's amazing grace.

Larry let Gracie set her own pace when they got home and took a long walk around the town house complex. When they were finished, he and Gracie sat on the back patio to watch the evening sky, set ablaze by the setting sun. Larry looped her leash around the arm of his wrought-iron chair and began to pray. He prayed for Ava and Hayden and each of the children at Suncoast. He prayed for the Trinity students, the patients at the VA, and the staff and caregivers working so hard to care for each one. As his prayers moved to the Canines for Christ dogs and volunteers, Gracie suddenly jumped up. Her tail stretched out behind her, and a low rumbling sound resonated through her chest—a sound Larry had never heard her make before.

"What is it, girl?" He stood up to see if he could detect whatever had captured her attention.

He followed her gaze to the next yard over where two large sandhill cranes were standing. At almost four feet tall, the cranes were the largest birds Gracie had ever seen up close, and she didn't know what to make of them.

"They're just birds. They don't mean you any ha—"

Too late. Driven by sheer instinct, Gracie charged after the birds, dragging the chair behind her. Her sudden reaction left Larry shocked and dumbfounded. At the first sound of the clattering chair, the birds spread their enormous wings and took flight. But Gracie kept charging ahead, no longer pursuing the birds but trying to get away from the loud, heavy monster that was chasing her through the neighbor's yard. She charged down the sidewalk with the wrought-iron chair scraping and screeching behind her.

"Gracie, stop!" Larry yelled.

"Gracie, come!" Susan shouted, running out the back door.

Gracie's head swung toward Larry, but when she caught sight of the chair, she picked up the pace. Larry and Susan charged after their dog, and several neighbors emerged from their back doors, some trying to intercept the Lab. But she was surprisingly fast, even towing a twenty-pound chair. After running past several more houses, Gracie took a hard right and jumped into the lake, freeing her leash from the chair, and leaving the wrought-iron monster on the shore. Gracie stayed in the water and waited for Larry. He didn't know if he wanted to laugh, cry, or jump in with her. He chose all three.

After checking to make sure she wasn't hurt, he picked up her leash and led her back home. Gracie hurried past the chair. Several neighbors saw them return and called out to see if Gracie was okay. When word spread that she was fine, cheers followed them home.

Larry hosed Gracie off, toweled her dry, and got her situated on her bed; then he went back to retrieve his chair. He suspected if it were up to Gracie, she would tell him to just throw the beast into the lake and leave it there.

CHAPTER THIRTEEN

LARRY SET HIS STEAMING CUP OF COFFEE on the coffee table and looked around the room filled with boxes. Most of the contents of the room had already been packed away. The only things left out in the living room were his Bible, journal, and pen. He sat back in his recliner and ran his foot back and forth over Gracie's back as she dozed. She raised sleepy eyes toward him, sighed, and turned over for a foot rub on her belly too. The one-year-old Lab had become a fixture in Larry's morning routine. She waited in the kitchen while he made coffee, followed him to his favorite chair, and lay at his feet while he prayed and read from the Bible. He couldn't imagine this sacred time without her—and prayed he wouldn't have to for a very long time. As far as he was concerned, the only drawback to loving a dog was its life span, which he felt wasn't nearly long enough.

He took another sip of coffee and shook off the heavy feeling. Gracie had celebrated her first birthday less than two weeks ago and had gotten a glowing report from the vet last week at her annual checkup. She was young and healthy and ready to take over for Cody, who had just started to show signs of slowing down. The vet said the retriever was healthy, just getting older and starting to develop some arthritis. Up until then, Larry had been feeling conflicted about retiring Cody. But God's timing had proven perfect as always. After today's visit to the veterans' hospital, Cody would retire, and Gracie would take his place as ambassador of Canines for Christ.

Larry picked up his pen and wrote a prayer in his journal. A prayer of thanksgiving for Cody and of grace and favor for Gracie, closing with these words.

This has always been your ministry, Lord. Continue to lead us and guide us. And continue to show your love to this world through these beautiful dogs.

Later that day, Larry escorted Cody through the main doors of the hospital. The happy Golden led the way down every corridor and into each room they visited, with Gracie following closely behind. Both dogs walked with their tails swaying and their ears raised. Gracie had visited the hospital campus close to a dozen times already, but Larry was acutely aware of the fact that the next time they visited, she wouldn't be following Cody—she would be stepping into his role. She would be the lead dog.

"Will you tell your dog to slow down a little?" Susan asked, panting slightly as she hurried to keep up with the excited Lab.

Larry normally held Gracie's leash, but today he had wanted

to walk with Cody. He glanced down and laughed at Gracie, who was trying to inch her way between him and Cody.

"Gracie, slow," he corrected.

They entered the main doors of The Cove and checked in with the receptionist, who fussed over Cody and Gracie. Larry and Susan visited several residents in their rooms and others who were gathered in common areas. Larry let everyone know that Cody was retiring, and several people thanked Cody for being such a nice dog and faithful visitor.

There was one special stop they had to make before leaving—the exercise room.

"Bernard! We brought Cody and Gracie to say hello to you."

An exuberant screech of joy erupted from the blind man's lips. Donna helped him off the exercise bike and led him to Larry, Susan, and two excited dogs. Gracie had quickly become as smitten with Bernard as Cody was, and Bernard had come to love Gracie with as much passion and volume as he loved Cody. He awkwardly wrapped his arms around the two of them.

"He just loves these visits," Donna said. "It's the only time he makes these sounds. These are your 'I love Cody and Gracie' words, aren't they, Mr. Bernard?"

The joy on Bernard's face said it all. Larry told Bernard and Donna that this was Cody's last visit—after today only Gracie would visit him.

"But Cody will always love you, Bernard. He has loved seeing you each week."

Bernard's bony hands searched for Cody's face. He placed a hand on each side of the dog's head and made a series of sounds only God and Cody could decipher. Larry wiped away a tear and said goodbye as Donna guided Bernard back to the exercise bike.

The foursome stopped in the spinal cord unit, then went to the main hospital wing, where they visited with staff, families, and patients. As they were entering the trauma unit, they ran into Cathy Marshall.

"Well, if it isn't Super Cody and his trusty sidekicks," she exclaimed. "I've been hearing rumors that this is your last day here, Cody. Is that right?"

Larry shared Cody's retirement plans and their intention to have Gracie take over.

"You've certainly earned an early retirement, Cody. But we don't want you to forget how much we love you and how much good you've done around here."

"I didn't think I would feel so emotional about this," Susan confessed when Cathy left.

Larry knew exactly what she meant. He was so happy that Cody would be a full-time buddy for little Luke, which would take a lot of energy for an eight-year-old dog. Larry didn't want to over-tax Cody with therapy work too. But he hadn't been prepared for the emotional reaction of what was turning into Cody's goodbye tour. He ruffled the dog's head, took a deep breath, and headed into the trauma unit. Several new patients had arrived from other hospitals, including an army sergeant named Joel with such severe injuries and burns that only his immediate family were permitted to enter his room. Larry and Susan could only wave to the young man's parents through the window—and have the dogs do Paws Up against the glass opening.

Joel appeared to be in a coma with nearly his entire body bandaged. His parents wore medical gowns and masks. Larry's heart broke for the man and his family. He hoped he would be able to visit with them soon—to offer a word of encouragement and a visit with Gracie. But for now, he would pray for them. Larry had seen many battered, bruised, and broken people in this hospital, but this young sergeant's injuries appeared more extensive than any he had seen before.

"God, have mercy on this man. Heal him. Sustain him. And grant peace to him and his family."

Larry and Susan continued down the corridor, but the young sergeant stayed in Larry's heart.

The rest of the day flew by. After they left the hospital, there was time for fun and Frisbee at the beach before driving Cody back home. When they arrived, Larry opened the door to let Cody jump from the car—something he had done countless times before. *This is it.* The finality of the moment caught in Larry's throat. He knelt down and put his head next to Cody's.

"Thank you," he whispered gratefully, tears streaming down his cheeks. "Thank you for trusting me. Thank you for starting this adventure with me. And thank you for letting God love others through you. You've done a great job, Cody."

Cody kissed Larry's tears away, spun in three tight circles, and then romped to the front door. He was ready to go home. And Luke's delighted squeal as he toddled toward his dog made Larry realize it was definitely time.

🐾

Two weeks later, Larry, Susan, and Gracie officially moved into their new house. "Gracie, welcome to your new home," Larry said, opening the front door. Gracie zoomed down the entryway, ran in circles in the family room, raced through the kitchen and dining room, and returned to the front door just as Larry closed it. "What do you think? Do you like it? But there's even more."

He led her through the family room and out the sliding glass doors to a covered patio and pool and a sizable backyard. Larry was looking forward to spending a lot of time outdoors, and by the way Gracie raced around the yard, he knew she would too. Larry and Susan slipped off their shoes, sat on the edge of the pool, and dangled their legs in the water.

"We did it, Susie," Larry sighed. "We rented our town house and moved into our dream house."

She bumped his shoulder with hers. "I can see us having big family dinners here and watching our grandkids swim in the pool. I can see us hosting Bible studies and Canines for Christ get-togethers. I'm so happy."

Splash!

"And so wet! Gracie!" Susan screeched.

Susan hadn't seen her change course and head straight for the water. It happened so fast Larry hadn't had time to warn her, but he found the entire situation so hilarious that he doubted he would have said anything to Susan even if he had. Gracie leapt into the pool with a most impressive, soaking dive. Quite pleased with herself, she swam to the steps, got out, squeezed herself between him and Susan, and shook vigorously. Effectively soaking them both—again. Susan tried to give Larry a stern look, but when Gracie shook a second time, Susan couldn't help but laugh.

Gracie headed toward the fence line and began sniffing with purpose. A few minutes later, she ran to him with something in her mouth. He could tell by the way she carried her tail that she was proud of herself.

"Whatcha got there, girl?"

Gracie held her mouth slightly open, but not far enough for Larry to see what was between her teeth. He reached his hand toward her and she turned her head slightly to the right. He tried again and she turned it slightly to the left.

"Gracie," he gently chided. "What do you have?" She looked forlornly at him, silently pleading not to take her treasure. Larry held his open palm under her mouth. "Drop."

She looked longingly from Larry to Susan before releasing her prize—a slobber-covered golf ball. One of many Larry imagined they would discover in their yard as more and more people played the course in the middle of the subdivision.

"Good girl, Gracie," Larry praised, deciding he would need to teach her that she would receive an even greater prize for bringing him the golf balls, as opposed to trying to chew on them. He went inside and opened a box of treats. When he came back out, he was glad Gracie was holding the golf ball in her mouth again.

"Drop," he instructed, and rewarded her with a treat when she did. He had a feeling "drop the golf ball for a treat" would become one of his dog's favorite games. But for now, he tossed the white ball over the fence.

At eight o'clock that night, as Larry and Susan unpacked another box in the kitchen, Gracie disappeared into their bedroom without their noticing.

"Where's Gracie?" Larry looked in various rooms, then called, "Susan, you have to come see this."

The young Lab was curled up inside the walk-in closet across from their bed. Larry had temporarily placed her bed there while they unpacked, but now it seemed perfect—Gracie's own little space. She opened one eye and looked at them. Her expression clearly said, *Keep it down, please. Someone needs some sleep.*

❧

The next morning, Larry and Gracie were sitting in what would be his new home office when his cell phone rang.

"Hi, Larry, this is Terry from Trinity. I'm sorry to call so early, but I'm hoping you might be able to help us."

"Of course, Terry."

"Earl passed away last night." Larry had not been prepared for that news. "His caregivers just let us know. The doctors are saying it was an aneurysm. Earl hadn't been well for a while, but none of us thought . . ." Terry's voice broke.

"Oh, Terry, I am so sorry. I liked Earl very much."

Cody the Wonder Dog. That was the name Earl bestowed on Cody the first time they met. Larry had just seen Earl during Cody's last visit to Trinity. The young man had stroked Cody's back for a good ten minutes, telling him what a good dog he was and how much he was going to miss him. He had even drawn a picture of Cody in a red cape with his title written in bright blue and taped it to the wall.

"We all liked Earl. I'm fearful our students are going to take this news very hard. I thought it might help if you brought Gracie so she could be available to anyone who needs a little extra support. I know it's last minute, but would you have any time today to stop by?"

Larry was already walking back to the bedroom to get ready. "Gracie and I will be there in an hour."

"You and Gracie will be where?" Susan asked after Larry hung up with Terry.

He filled her in on the heartbreaking situation, then hurried to shower and finish getting ready. Susan was watching Luke all day, so he and Gracie would go by themselves.

A wave of grief washed over Larry at the thought of the pain Earl's family was feeling right now. *Oh Father, help them through this difficult time.*

Terry met Larry and Gracie at the front door of Trinity and led them into a large multipurpose room where more than two dozen students were huddled in small groups. Several were crying, some were rocking back and forth, and a few were wandering around the room looking confused and unsure.

"Earl died," a woman named Stephanie told Larry. She threw her arms around him, and then knelt to hug Gracie.

Ed scooted next to Gracie and patted his lap. When she responded, Ed folded himself over her.

While Stephanie and Ed huddled by Gracie, Terry softly filled Larry in. "We told the students that Earl's heart got hurt very badly and the doctors couldn't make it better. We told them he died—and said that's what happens when someone's heart stops beating, their lungs stop breathing, and they don't move or think anymore. We know it will take a while for all of this to sink in, but we wanted to give everyone a chance to process it together."

"Thank you for calling," Larry said, grateful for the opportunity to both mourn Earl and offer comfort and hope to his friends and their caregivers.

"Can I pet Gracie?" Leslie asked.

Ed was hesitant to let go of Gracie, but he finally made space for Leslie too.

"Chaplain Larry," a middle-aged man named Thomas tapped

him on the back, then maneuvered his wheelchair so he faced Larry. "Why didn't God save Earl?"

Larry hadn't been prepared for the question—even though it was one he had asked God many times over the years about different situations and people. He inhaled deeply, asked God to speak through him, then said, "I don't know, Thomas."

He wanted to give the frail-looking man an answer. But if there was one thing Larry had learned during his own seasons of suffering and grief, as well as walking alongside others facing death, loss, illness, and injury, sometimes—oftentimes—there are no answers. Only opportunities. Opportunities to grieve, to trust, to choose love over fear, and to find a way to be content without an answer. To heal and hope and live in spite of not ever knowing the why behind the suffering is perhaps the greatest act of faith someone can ever show.

"I am so sorry Earl died," Larry said, placing his arm around Thomas. "And I know that God loves Earl very much and that he loves you very much too, and he wants to help you through this hard time."

"Does God love *me*?" Leslie asked.

"Yes, he loves you very much," Larry answered. By now, many of the students had gathered around him. Larry looked into each person's face and went around the circle. "And God loves you, and you, and you." Gracie made a slow circuit through the crowd. As she ministered with her presence, Larry asked Thomas if he knew about heaven.

"Heaven is where God lives, right, Chaplain Larry?"

Larry smiled and gently squeezed the man's shoulder. "You're right. Heaven is where God's throne is." Larry addressed all of them. "Heaven is the most perfect and beautiful place you could ever imagine. It's perfect because God is there. And his Son, Jesus, is there. And one day all of his children will be there with him. That's what happens when God's children die. When our bodies," Larry patted his arms and stomach and legs, "stop working and we die, our souls—the part of us deep inside that makes us who we really are—that part goes to heaven to live forever with God. And you want to know something wonderful that the Bible tells us about heaven?"

Heads nodded and several people shouted, "Yes!"

"There is no sickness in heaven. No sadness. No one feels sad or angry or lonely. No one gets hurt in heaven. No one dies in heaven." Larry lowered his voice to a whisper. "And guess what."

"What?"

"We get to see Jesus in heaven. In fact, I bet Jesus is welcoming Earl with a big hug right now."

"Will Earl have to take his medicine in heaven?" Leslie asked.

"No one has to take medicine in heaven."

"Will I have my chair in heaven?" Thomas asked.

His question made Larry tear up. "No, Thomas. You won't need that chair in heaven. In fact, the Bible says we will get brand-new bodies. That means we will be able to run and jump and . . ." And then the responses began.

"Dance!"

"Twirl!"

"Kick!"

"Ski!"

"Walk!"

Yes, all of those things and even more, Larry thought with a smile.

"It's okay to be sad about having to say goodbye for now to

Earl. You will miss him—we will all miss him very much. But it's also good to think about heaven and all the wonderful things Earl is getting to do. But do you want to know the most amazing thing of all?"

Everyone looked eagerly at Larry.

"Jesus will be in heaven with us, but he is also with us now."

A few heads turned, looking around.

"We can't see Jesus with the eyes we have now, but he is here. He is as real as the oxygen we are breathing. Can you see the oxygen going in your nose?" Heads shook.

"But is it there?" Heads nodded.

"We can't see Jesus but he is here, and he wants to be as close to us as Gracie is. Just like Gracie wants to sit with you and listen to you, Jesus wants to be with you and listen to you too. In fact, we can talk to him right now. Would you like to pray with me?"

Once again, heads nodded.

"Dear heavenly Father, thank you for letting us know Earl. We are so sad that we won't be able to see him anymore, but we thank you that he is with you now. Earl's friends miss him so much. Give them hope and comfort them with your love. Help us to think about heaven and to remember all the wonderful promises you've given us about living forever with you. We ask this in Jesus' name, amen."

Larry heard a sniffle behind him and was touched to see Terry wiping her eyes.

Thank you, she mouthed.

Larry and Gracie spent the next two hours visiting classrooms, hugging bereaved staff and students, and making themselves available to anyone who wanted to talk, hug and pet Gracie, pray, or just sit. By the end of his visit, Larry was emotionally drained, yet spiritually full. When he got home, Larry jotted a note in his journal.

Talk to Terry about starting a Canines for Christ Bible study for students at Trinity.

Just writing down the idea made his heart beat a little faster. *Thank you, Earl.*

CHAPTER FOURTEEN

"I CAN'T BELIEVE HOW MUCH BETTER my ankle feels after getting the cortisone shot last week."

Larry and Susan were enjoying a pleasant February day in the midseventies. Even though the influx of seasonal tourists meant more traffic on the roads and longer waits at restaurants, Larry certainly understood the appeal of Florida in winter. It was hard to imagine living anywhere else.

"How long did the doctor say the shot will last?"

Susan threw a tennis ball for Gracie, and she ran off and lunged into a bush in hot pursuit.

"He said it could last anywhere from a few weeks to several months. Here's hoping for several months."

Gracie pranced her way back and dropped the ball at Larry's feet.

"*I* throw it, but she brings it back to *you*," Susan teased. "You are such a daddy's girl, Gracie."

Larry didn't even try to argue. It was true. He had no doubt that Gracie loved Susan, but he was the one Gracie followed around the house; he was the one she ran to first when they came home; and he was the one whose feet she sat by every night. And he loved it. Larry threw the next ball and Gracie came prancing back with . . . a golf ball.

"Wrong ball, Gracie," Larry teased. But in keeping with what had become a very familiar routine, Larry exchanged the golf ball for a treat and threw it back over the fence.

Susan shook her head. "She's trained you very well."

🐾

Larry had just turned into the parking lot of the VA hospital for what he anticipated would be several hours of visits when his cell phone rang.

"Hi, Larry, it's Darleen. I hope I'm not interrupting you, but I just had to tell you the most amazing story."

Darleen and her beautiful Golden Retriever, Passion, had been volunteering with Canines for Christ for over a year. She had reached out to Larry about volunteering soon after she had retired from full-time nursing. And while it was her dog who was named Passion, Darleen's passion for encouraging patients in nursing homes and medical facilities was obvious to everyone who met her.

"You aren't interrupting at all," Larry assured her. "It's great to hear from you."

"You will never believe what just happened," the woman began, her voice breathy from excitement. "Do you remember me telling you about Glenn at the nursing home Passion and I have been visiting? The man confined to a wheelchair who loves to do impersonations and sing?"

Larry did remember.

"Well, I've had a soft spot for that man ever since I met him. He's just always so full of life and sass—guess he reminds me a bit of myself," she said with a chuckle.

"Anyway, Glenn loves Passion. He loves petting her, he loves singing to her, and I love getting to see him smile. But I've never really understood my connection to him, and we've never talked about his past.

"Well, as I was walking out today, I met a woman who's known Glenn since he was a boy. She recognized Passion from his description and thanked me for brightening Glenn's day. Then she said, 'It's been hard for Glenn's family since his devastating lawn mower accident forty years ago.'

"Larry, my mouth dropped open! I started peppering her with questions. 'Was Glenn in a coma for a long time?' She said yes. And then we both said together, 'But the doctors didn't expect him to survive.'"

Darleen's voice rose an octave. "Larry, Glenn was my patient forty years ago! Can you believe it? I never imagined that he was the same Glenn I had cared for all those years ago. Isn't God just wonderful that he would bring us back together like that?"

Larry nodded, even though Darleen couldn't see him.

"Well, I ran back in that room and hugged Glenn's neck and told him I had been his nurse after the accident. We both got a little tearful. But then he looked at me and said, 'All those doctors said I wasn't supposed to live, but I sure fooled them, huh?' He sure did. Oh Larry, thank you for saying yes to God and starting this ministry. I feel like God just gave me a precious gift—one that I wouldn't have gotten without this ministry. Thank you."

"Thank *you*," Larry said, overwhelmed by her story and by God's grace. Before heading into the hospital, Larry prayed, "Thank you, Father, for allowing me to play a role in this wonderful plan of yours. This ministry of grace and of your presence." Then he clipped Gracie's leash to her collar and said, "All right girl, let's go to work."

They started in the spinal care wing, then walked over to The Cove to make the round of visits, including one with Bernard.

It had taken Bernard a while to adjust to Gracie. He had loved burying his face in Cody's long, silky hair, but since Gracie was a Labrador Retriever, her hair was shorter and coarse, which felt different on his skin. But during one of their early visits with Gracie, Donna placed Bernard's hands on the Lab's ears and showed him how soft they were. That was all it took. From that point on, the first thing Bernard did when he got within an arm's reach of Gracie was run his fingers over her ears. Now, when Gracie approached Bernard, she immediately sat and put her head next to him.

Forty-five minutes later, Larry and Gracie walked to the psychiatric ward in the main hospital. They had been there several times before. To Larry, the needs in the psychiatric ward and trauma units often felt the weightiest and most intense, especially a need for hope. A longing for a glimmer of light in the midst of crushing darkness.

It was a need Gracie seemed divinely appointed to meet as she interacted with men and women so lost in their present circumstances that they couldn't imagine—let alone see—any hope that tomorrow would be different. But oftentimes after meeting

Gracie, something extraordinary would occur—their tomorrows would suddenly hold the possibility of hope, even if it was just the hope of seeing her again.

Larry knew he would never tire of witnessing the transformation. So when he spotted a man sitting by himself in the common area where higher functioning patients played games and watched TV, he asked God to bring hope through his dog once again.

Gracie walked up to the man—who appeared to be in his sixties—sitting by himself.

"Who are you?" he asked her.

"This is Gracie, and I'm Larry. What's your name?"

"Fig Newton."

Larry assumed it was a nickname, but when the man offered no other information, Larry smiled and shook his hand. "It's nice to meet you, Fig Newton. Gracie and I just wanted to come over and say hi and let you know that God loves you and that your life matters to him—and to us."

Fig Newton placed a large, rough hand on Gracie's back and squinted.

"She a nice dog?"

"She's a very nice dog," Larry assured him. "And she really seems to like you. See how calm she is and how she's looking at you? She feels safe with you."

"Feels safe with *me*?" the heavyset man marveled, before proceeding to tell Larry about the forty years he spent working the carnival circuits.

"I done some things I ain't proud of—some bad things that put me here. I reckon I won't ever be gettin' out. My mama told me 'bout God when I was young. But I'm sure he wants nothing to do with me now." The man seemed to search Gracie's eyes for some hidden truth buried there. He scratched her chin. "You really think God can love the likes of me?"

"God loves all people," Larry said, looking in Fig Newton's eyes. "And I know for a fact God loves you because he says so in the Bible. He said he loves the whole world—and you're part of the world, aren't you?"

Fig Newton nodded.

"There's a verse in the Bible that says that God loves the world so much that he sent his Son, Jesus, to the earth to live the life we couldn't, so that when we trust in him, he forgives all the wrong we've done and gives us eternal life and hope."

Fig Newton's face softened as he watched Gracie, so Larry kept going. "Would you like to talk to God? Gracie will sit with you, as I pray, then you can pray to him afterward if you'd like. How does that sound?"

"I suppose that sounds okay."

Larry leaned forward. "Father, thank you for loving us, even though we sin and do bad things. Thank you letting me and Gracie meet Fig Newton. Let him know how much you love him. He feels bad about some of the things he has done. Please forgive him and let him feel your peace."

Larry was pleasantly surprised when the man began to pray.

"God, I, uh, well, I done some bad stuff—I s'pose you know what I done. But I don't want to do those things no more. I want to have the peace Mr. Larry was talkin' about, and if it ain't too much trouble, um . . . would you forgive me?"

Larry's heart was beating so hard he feared it was visible through his shirt. After Fig Newton's prayer, Larry pulled a Bible and a pamphlet titled *Steps to Peace with God* out of the Canines for Christ briefcase he usually carried with him—for just such an occasion.

Fig Newton stared as though what Larry was offering him was made of gold.

"For *me*? To keep? I can give 'em back to you when you come back."

"No, no," Larry assured. "These are a gift. From me—and Gracie—to you. To keep. We want you to read and learn more about God and about how much he loves you. And when I come back, we can talk about what you've read and any questions you have. How does that sound?"

There were tears in the former carnival worker's eyes. "That sounds mighty fine."

After visiting with a few other patients and two security guards, Larry led Gracie back up to the trauma unit. He was getting tired, but Gracie didn't show any signs of slowing down. There was definitely one person they needed to see before leaving for the day— Joel, the young army sergeant. Even though they could only see him through the glass the first few weeks of his recovery, Larry made it a priority to do so. As soon as they were cleared to go inside his room, they learned more about Joel and what had happened to him.

The young man had sustained burns to sixty percent of his body when rockets hit the Humvee he and several members of his unit were riding in. The blast killed three of the men instantly, and while Joel was thought to have been killed, he miraculously survived. As Larry got to know Joel's parents while their son recovered from his extensive injuries, he learned that their son was the second most severely injured army soldier to have survived since the Iraq War had begun. He was blind, had sustained severe head trauma, had lost his right leg and four fingers on his left hand, and had extensive burns all over his body—but he had survived. When

Joel emerged from his eighty-day coma, Larry realized the young man was determined to live each new day he had been given with purpose and with as much joy as he could muster.

"We had to say hello to one of Gracie's favorite friends," Larry said as he entered Joel's hospital room.

His mother welcomed Larry and Gracie. Larry led Gracie to Joel's bed and picked her up to lie beside him.

"She was pulling me down the hall to get to you."

Joel stroked Gracie's back, and his eyes twinkled with amusement.

"Had to pull the old man pretty hard to get him to move fast, huh, Gracie?"

Joel reminded Larry of Charlie. Both men were somehow able, in spite of their severe injuries and pain, to maintain their sense of humor. It seemed as if they had found a way to use humor as a weapon against despair and hopelessness.

Larry and Gracie spent close to twenty minutes with Joel and his parents, trading stories, laughing, and talking about the future—including Joel's plan to skydive someday. His mother wasn't keen on that idea, but Larry had no doubt, if there was a way for Joel to accomplish his goal, he would make it happen.

After a quick lunch, Larry and Gracie headed to ManorCare Nursing and Rehabilitation Center, where they would team up with Laura and Chloe. This new team had been to the nursing home two times already, and Larry was impressed at how quickly Laura was fitting in. She was a bit tentative interacting with the staff and residents, but Larry knew that she would grow more comfortable with more experience. He and Susan encouraged Laura to consider sharing her story of finding hope in the midst of her suffering with the residents. Larry believed that Laura's story had the potential to positively affect many people in a way his own story never could. That was one of many things he loved about the ministry—how God worked through the diversity of people's experiences. How he brought together people with different backgrounds, family situations, faith journeys, and life experiences, along with dogs in all shapes, sizes, colors, and ages, to minister to a diverse and hurting world.

Laura and Chloe were waiting outside ManorCare. "We are ready to go to work!"

Chloe and Gracie nosed each other's ears and gave an enthusiastic bounce. Larry was tired from the intense hours he had already spent at the hospital, but as soon as they stepped into ManorCare's large common room and he saw faces light up with smiles, a renewed energy surged through him. This was what he was meant to do, and by the look on Laura's face, she was feeling the same way.

For the next two hours, they intermingled with three dozen residents and staff. Laura and Chloe were representing Canines for Christ well, and Larry was proud to serve beside her. When it was time to say goodbye for the day, Larry thanked Laura for a job well done. That evening after dinner, Larry relaxed by the pool as the sun dipped below the tree line. Gracie walked the perimeter of the yard while he stretched out in his chaise lounge, closed his eyes, and listened to the sounds of the evening—the soft buzz of insects, the gentle rustling of palm fronds in the breeze, and the croak of a frog nearby. Larry was embraced by the peaceful moment.

The moment was abruptly—and loudly—interrupted by ferocious barking. Gracie was frantically patrolling the pool deck—barking and glaring at something.

"What in the world is the matter, Gracie?" He had never heard his dog sound so aggressive. Something was upsetting her.

Something made her feel threatened—or awakened an instinct to protect her pack.

I don't see anything in the pool, he thought. He tried to quiet Gracie, but she was determined to make her displeasure known. Maybe whatever she was seeing was lower. Larry followed Gracie around the pool deck, hunching over and staring out into the yard.

"What in the world are you doing?" Susan said, walking out the back door.

Larry tried to explain over Gracie's deep, incessant barking. A moment later she stopped and stared into the corner of the pool and barked even louder. Whatever she saw was causing the hair on the back of her neck to rise.

Larry and Susan both peered into the water.

A tiny little frog peered back.

"Is that what you've been making all this noise about?"

Larry shook his head. Leave it to his sweet-tempered therapy dog to lose her mind over a tiny little frog. He cupped his hand around the nickel-sized amphibian and released it through the fence. Gracie followed him, barking and grumbling the whole way. Larry held out his empty hands. "See? The frog is all gone. We're safe now."

Gracie sniffed his hands from fingers to wrist. She stuck her nose through the fence and sniffed. She rounded the pool, listening and smelling for any sign of the intruder. Finally, satisfied that all was well once again, she stretched out next to the railing for the pool steps and sighed. Guarding a pool was hard work.

❧

A few days later Larry got a call from a woman in Pinellas County who wanted to join the ministry. Karla had recently met one of the Canines for Christ teams at St. Joseph's Hospital, where her niece was battling cancer.

"The little dog we met—I think his name was Ditto—brought such a big smile to my niece's face. He was the sweetest little thing curled up in her bed. It was the first real smile I've seen on her face since her surgery."

Larry smiled at the image of the little black-haired terrier bringing joy to a young cancer patient.

Karla continued. "I came home later that day and looked at my tricolored terrier, Buddy, and thought maybe we could help bring smiles to other people's faces. I know you're based in Tampa, and we're over in Indian Rocks Beach, but I would love to join your ministry."

Larry loved the idea of expanding Canines for Christ into another county. Indian Rocks Beach was only an hour's drive away. It would be easy for him to meet Karla and Buddy and give the terrier the Canine Good Citizen test since Larry was now an AKC Canine Good Citizen evaluator. Becoming certified as an evaluator had helped streamline the Canines for Christ volunteer process. He and Karla set up a meeting for the following week.

"With the addition of Karla and Buddy, we'll be able to take Canines for Christ across Tampa Bay and share God's love through our dogs with even more people," Larry told Susan later that evening as they prepared three new volunteer kits.

"That brings our total volunteer teams to fifty-four," Susan said. She had just restocked their supply of vests, T-shirts, prayer cards, and training materials so she knew exactly how many teams they currently had.

More than fifty teams in just over two years. It was both a great honor and a weighty responsibility. Between meeting with prospective volunteers, evaluating potential dogs, conducting new volunteer training, making visits, ordering and mailing out supplies, and making time for his own family, Larry was busier than when he had been working full time. And yet, as he and Susan finished boxing up the new volunteer kits, he had never felt more fulfilled or been more certain that he was doing exactly what he was put on this earth to do.

"It really is going well, isn't it?"

"Better than I ever could have dreamed," Larry said. "Not only do we have teams in nursing homes, hospitals, cancer centers, schools, and special-needs centers, we're forming relationships with law enforcement agencies, libraries, and local churches. It's incredible."

The two sat in silence for several minutes, just taking it all in. But there was something he wanted to discuss with Susan before they called it a night.

"You have a special birthday coming up later this year," he said, folding his hands on the table, "and given how busy our lives have become, I think we should take a trip to celebrate. Just the two of us going somewhere to reconnect, rest, and enjoy being together."

"Did you have a destination in mind?"

Her eyes twinkled and cheeks flushed with excitement. He wanted to tease her and suggest another service trip to rebuild a storm-ravaged area. But she had been talking about another place for so long that he couldn't prolong the moment any longer.

"I was thinking a week in Saint Bart's."

Susan clapped her hands over her mouth, then hugged him. "Really?"

Larry gave her a quick kiss. "You and me on a French Caribbean island for a week? Absolutely!"

They spent the next two hours looking at hotels, restaurants, and itineraries online. When they were done, they had booked their airline tickets, hotel, and rental car—and made a reservation with the pet-sitter—for the first week of October.

"Seven months has never seemed so long," Susan sighed later that night while she and Larry got ready for bed. "How will I ever wait that long to get to Saint Bart's?"

Thankfully for Susan, the months leading up to their trip were so busy with ministry activities and the birth of three more grand-children that the time passed quickly, and they were soon on their way to Saint Bart's. They celebrated Susan's sixtieth birth-day week savoring delicious meals, exploring lush green hillsides, taking countless photos of jewel-blue water, and visiting lots of small shops and markets in search of souvenirs for their daughters and granddaughters—including Brooke's one-year-old daughter, Lexi, and Tara's infant twins, Jessica and Sophie. With the excep-tion of some death-defying tight curves while driving and the red-eye flight back, it was a perfect vacation. After an abbreviated night's sleep, they were on their way to the pet-sitter's to pick up Gracie.

"I can't wait to see my girl," Larry exclaimed on the way.

"Hey!" Susan protested.

"I mean, I can't wait to see my *four-legged* girl." His blue eyes twinkled mischievously. "After all, I've spent a whole week with my two-legged one in a Caribbean paradise, and I need a break."

Susan huffed and feigned outrage. Larry squeezed her hand. "You know I'm kidding. I had a wonderful time in Saint Bart's with you."

"I did too," Susan agreed, then added, "but I'm also ready to see Gracie. I really missed her."

Larry was grateful that Gracie had enjoyed her own vacation with her pet-sitter, Miriam. Gracie loved staying with Miriam, and Larry knew she was being treated like royalty. And yet, he also knew his dog would be as happy to see him as he would be to see her.

They pulled into Miriam's driveway and Larry hurried from the car. He rang the doorbell and heard Gracie's deep, throaty bark. Miriam cracked the door open, and Gracie opened it the rest of the way with her head. She did a happy dance, with her tail swinging and body wiggling. Larry dropped to his knees inside the door and hugged his dog to the tune of delighted whines and whimpers.

Fifteen minutes later, they were heading for home. Larry couldn't wait to sit in his favorite spot on their sectional sofa with Gracie at his feet, flip on the TV, and take a post-vacation nap. He glanced in the rearview mirror and saw her smiling. Larry squeezed Susan's hand. His heart was full and his mind renewed and ready to begin the fourth year of the Canines for Christ ministry. They took Gracie home, and after spending several minutes on the floor with her, rubbing her belly and assuring her they weren't leaving again anytime soon, Susan went to take a shower. Minutes later, Gracie walked to her favorite napping spot by the glass doors and lay down with a sigh. Larry channel surfed to a golf game, leaned back against the sofa cushion, and closed his eyes. All was right with his world.

Until it wasn't.

CHAPTER FIFTEEN

"SUSAN!" Larry screamed at the sight of his wife's lifeless body sprawled out on their bathroom floor.

Gracie's frantic barking had jarred him awake moments earlier after dozing off in front of the TV, and yet now he was in the middle of a living nightmare.

"Susan!" he screamed again, dropping to his knees beside her.

Gracie's frenzied barks turned to mournful whines. The skin above Susan's right eyebrow was turning a deep purple. Her lips were tight. Her eyes closed. *What happened?* Larry looked around the bathroom for clues and tried to make sense of the scene. She had gone to take a shower; the water was off; she was in her robe; the hairdryer was on the counter. Bile rose in Larry's throat at the image that formed in his mind. His wife's beautiful face hitting the granite sink counter before falling backward against the tile floor.

Gracie nudged his shoulder, bringing his attention back to Susan.

Think, Larry, he commanded himself.

The tile floor was ice cold. He put his arms under Susan's shoulders and pulled her out of the bathroom and onto the warmer bedroom carpet. Gracie anxiously paced in a circle. When she nudged Susan's right hand with her nose, Larry noticed a pool of blood forming under Susan's head.

"Oh, God. What do I do?" he half cried, half prayed.

Susan's face was turning chalky gray. *She can't breathe.* Larry tried to open her mouth, but her jaw was locked. Gracie whined.

Turn her on her side.

Whether the thought was a memory from first-aid training he had received years ago or a divine command, Larry couldn't tell, but he wasted no time obeying. As he gently lifted Susan onto her side, blood began trickling from her mouth.

"Oh God, help us," he prayed through tears. "I can't lose her! I can't . . ."

Gracie lay down and leaned her head against Susan's stomach. Larry patted his pockets. His cell phone was on the coffee table in the family room.

"Gracie, stay with her," he said. Gracie looked up at him, then gently nuzzled her nose back into Susan's side. She was doing for Susan what she had been trained to do for others—provide a steady calm in the midst of an emotional storm. And Gracie's calm felt like a lifeline to Larry, a reminder that he wasn't alone.

He picked up his phone and shakily punched in 911.

It rang only once before someone picked up.

"Help!" he shouted, his voice thick with fear as his eyes met Gracie's. "We need help."

The next ten minutes were a blur of tears, terror, and prayer as Larry awaited the paramedics. He kept feeling for Susan's pulse, but it was getting harder and harder to find. Gracie stayed pressed against Susan's side, never taking her eyes off Larry. Her presence was a lifeline of comfort in a situation that felt anything but comforting. "God, please help us. Please help Susan. Don't let her die." How was this happening? And *what* had happened? Susan had been so healthy. Animated. Alive.

Loud banging startled Larry—and Gracie. She charged the door, barking ferociously. "I'll be right back, Susie."

He ran to the door, fumbled with the lock, then threw it open.

"Back there!" he shouted to the paramedics, pointing to the hallway back to the bedroom.

Five EMS responders quickly got to Susan. Larry and Gracie followed them, but they were stopped in the doorway by a man holding a clipboard.

"I need to get some information from you so we can best help your wife," he said. "And do you have a leash for your dog?"

Larry was confused. Why would he ask about Gracie's leash? His dog didn't need a walk. His wife needed help. She was dying!

"Help her," he squeaked out.

The paramedic assured Larry they were helping Susan, but reiterated that he needed Larry to answer some questions about Susan's health, and to put Gracie—who was barking and running around the first responders—on a leash to help her calm down. Larry got Gracie's leash and clipped it to her collar, then gave the paramedic Susan's medical history. She suffered from occasional and debilitating migraines and had a seizure when she was twenty-one.

"But she only had that one. And since she was doing so well, her doctor took her off the seizure medication about five years ago. Wait, do you think she had a seizure?"

"We'll let the doctors figure all of that out once she's at the hospital."

"We need an airlift!" Larry heard shouted from the bedroom.

Everything suddenly moved quickly. Susan was loaded on a stretcher and wheeled out the front door.

"Susan, I'm here," Larry shouted, touching her arm. "I love you."

As soon as she was placed in the back of the ambulance, Larry watched them hook her up to several IVs. Curious neighbors were standing in their driveways.

"There's not enough room to land the helicopter on the street, so we're going to drive her to the entrance of the subdivision and meet the chopper there. We need to get her to the trauma unit."

Larry nodded, trying to absorb the information.

"Can I ride with her?"

"You can follow us to St. Joseph's."

Why couldn't he wake up from this nightmare? I just want Susan . . .

"Larry?"

His next-door neighbors were beside him, asking if they could take Gracie. Larry looked down, surprised to find Gracie at his side, her leash in his hand. The dog had grown so quiet that he forgot she was there. He handed her leash to the man—whose name he couldn't remember. But the moment he released her leash, a rush of panic overtook him. He wanted her back. He needed her. But he also wanted her safe. And right now his house wasn't the safest place for her. He felt so helpless with Susan, but at least he could ensure Gracie was safe.

"Thank you," he choked out. "I'll come by and get her after . . . I'll get her when . . ."

"We will keep her as long as you need us to," the woman said. "You just focus on Susan. We've got Gracie."

Judy and Kevin. Their names came rushing back to Larry. He kneeled down and hugged his dog.

"Thank you, girl," he whispered, his tears wetting her head. "I'll be back soon." *And please, God, let Susan return with me*, he begged.

The ambulance door slammed shut, jolting Larry into action. He ran inside and grabbed his keys, wallet, phone, and shoes, got in the car, and followed the ambulance to where a helicopter sat waiting in the large circular entrance to the subdivision. As they loaded Susan into the air ambulance, Larry breathed a prayer. *God, take care of her. Please let her come through this. Please don't let me lose her.* The familiar route to the hospital—one he had taken countless times with Cody and Gracie—now felt oddly foreign. His hands shook. His insides jumped.

At the first stoplight Larry pulled out his phone. He needed to let Brooke and Tara know what had happened. He tried to keep his voice steady, but it was hard to contain his emotions as he told them. They said they would meet him at the hospital. Next, he called Ellie—Susan's good friend from their Bible study small group. She said she would let everyone know what was going on and ask them to pray. A short time later, and without a clear memory of how he had gotten there, Larry pulled into the parking lot at St. Joseph's trauma unit. He ran inside and was taken to a waiting room, where he was shocked to find two friends from his small group.

"How did you . . . ?"

"Ellie called. We were having lunch across the street and came right over."

Larry embraced them, grateful for their presence, and—as they started to pray for Susan—even more grateful for their prayers. Within a half hour, Brooke and Tara and other members of the prayer group joined Larry in the waiting room.

Several hours later a doctor in pale green scrubs came to the waiting room to update Larry, Brooke, and Tara.

"She is stable and was awake for a brief moment." Larry's relief was so intense, he wanted to sink into a chair, but he remained on his feet. "At this point we don't know if she had a heart attack, a stroke, or a seizure. But we do know that she sustained severe head trauma and is bleeding from her brain. The brain bleed is our biggest concern. We are monitoring her closely and will need to keep her here for several days. Once the test results come back, we'll know better what happened, but for now we are focusing on the head trauma."

"Will she be okay?" Larry asked.

"We won't know for a while," the doctor answered honestly. "It's hard to predict with severe head trauma. For now, let's get the test results back and give her brain some time to heal. We'll know more over time."

The doctor's tone was reassuring, but Larry had seen enough head trauma patients over the years to know that Susan might never be the same. *If she wakes up at all, she may never walk again, never talk again, never sit with me by pool. Never hold my hand. Never hold her grandchildren. Oh God, help me be strong for her.*

Larry spent a restless night in the recliner in Susan's room. Between the constant noise and activity in the hallway, the bright monitors, worry consuming him, and the need to check on her every few minutes, he slept only in short increments. Every time he closed his eyes, he saw Susan motionless on the bathroom floor and jolted awake.

Susan had roused a few times throughout the night, but she was disoriented and fearful. Thankfully, she had been sleeping peacefully for the past few hours. As the October sun rose, Larry tried to pray. But no words came. He had prayed at countless bedsides, but when his wife needed his prayers the most, he had none to offer. He managed two words: "God, help." He needed to be strong for Susan, but he was feeling weak and helpless.

"Larry?"

Pastor Matthew. *It's Sunday—isn't it? What is he doing here? Shouldn't he be at church?*

Larry tried to get up, but his legs felt weighted down. Pastor Matthew walked over and put his hand on Larry's shoulder.

"Larry, I am so very sorry. I don't want to intrude. I just wanted to come by to see if there was anything I could do for you and Susan."

Larry's bottom lip quivered. His hands began to tremble.

"Pray," he whispered.

Matthew leaned over Larry and prayed. He asked God to heal and protect Susan, to fill Larry with strength and peace, to comfort their family, and to mobilize their friends and their church to be the hands and feet of Jesus to them. Tears streamed down Larry's cheeks, sobs of release, exhaustion, and gratitude, as Matthew's arms steadied him and provided refuge.

"Larry? Pastor Matthew?"

Susan's weak, raspy voice was the most beautiful sound Larry had ever heard. He grabbed her hand and told her how much he loved her.

"I'm so sorry."

"Oh my love, you don't have anything to be sorry for. We are just so happy to see those eyes of yours and hear your voice. Pastor Matthew came by to pray for you." Larry looked at his watch, then at their pastor. "Don't you have to get to church?"

"Oh, it'll do the deacons good to sweat it out a bit—make them think one of them will have to give an impromptu message," he said with a smile.

In the midst of such trauma and fear, it felt so good to laugh—even for a moment. Matthew prayed again for both of them before he left. A few minutes later, Susan's doctor came in with her test results. Susan had suffered a grand mal seizure, which caused her to lose consciousness and hit her head. They would treat the seizures with the same medication she had been taking for decades, but the more pressing concern was her head trauma.

"The bleeding and swelling will dissipate over time," the neurologist explained, "but it will take a while before we know any long-term effects she might have. We will keep her here a few more days and continue to monitor her closely, and if she continues to improve, she'll be able to go home. But she will need someone to stay with her at all times for the first several weeks."

"We will do whatever it takes," Larry assured him.

Susan was sleeping when Brooke arrived.

"I told Tara I'd take the first shift. We figured you'd need to check on Gracie and get a few things at the house—and if you can, maybe even take a nap in a real bed."

Larry embraced Brooke, gently kissed the top of his wife's head, and headed home. But as he reached his front door, he froze, haunted by the horrible memories of the last twenty-four hours.

I can't go in there. I can't face seeing the bedroom. The bathroom. Bile rose in his throat.

His cell phone rang.

"Larry, it's Ellie. Deb and I are at the front of your subdivision. May we come by? We've brought cleaning supplies. We don't want you to have to deal with all of that."

Larry nodded before realizing they needed a verbal answer.

"Yes, that would be—" his words caught in his throat—"that would be . . . yes, thank you."

Larry unlocked the front door for them, then walked over to the neighbors' house to get Gracie. Her bark felt like a hug to his soul. She burst through the open door and pressed herself against his legs. Larry thanked Judy and Kevin for their generosity and kindness, filled them in on Susan's condition, assured them he would call them if he needed anything, then took Gracie back home. Ellie's and Deb's cars were in the driveway.

Thank you, Father, he breathed. He wasn't ready to enter the house yet, so he took Gracie into the backyard and they sat at the edge of the pool. She leaned against him and sighed, and that was all it took. The dam holding back the flood of emotions broke for the second time that morning and Larry wept. Gracie didn't move. Larry began to focus on Gracie's rhythmic breaths, then he began to focus on his own. *Inhale. Exhale. Inhale. Exhale.*

Inhale—*When I am afraid,*
Exhale—*I will trust in you.*
Inhale—*When I am afraid,*
Exhale—*I will trust in you.*

Larry had heard of breath prayers before but had never experienced the power of them like he did now. Inhaling and exhaling truth calmed his soul like nothing else had.

The sliding glass door opened and Ellie stuck her head out.

"We're all done. Everything is cleaned up, and dinner is in the fridge. We'll be back tomorrow with some groceries, and our church will have meals coming for you every day for the next several weeks. You just focus on Susan, and let us deal with the cooking and cleaning and shopping."

Larry walked into his house and hugged the thoughtful women. They shared tears and prayers, and then left. Larry fed Gracie and opened some mail. But he knew he couldn't put off the thing he was dreading most. He needed a change of clothes, and he needed to pack a bag for Susan, which meant he had to walk into their bedroom.

His hands were cold and clammy. He took several steps toward the room, then stopped.

Gracie barking at the door . . .

Silence coming from the bedroom . . .

The heart-sinking realization that something was wrong . . .

Susan's lifeless body . . .

Blood . . .

Panic . . .

Gracie's head nudged Larry's hand, bringing him back to the present. She whined and scooted closer.

"You saved her," he spoke aloud—to God and to his dog. He knelt down and hugged Gracie. "You woke me up. You heard her fall, and you woke me up. Thank you."

Larry took a deep breath. Then another. He was resolved to focus on God's provision. Gracie took the lead and stepped into the bedroom, and Larry followed. She jumped up on the bed and he sat beside her, rubbing his hand down her back, over her head, down her chest. He sat petting his dog until exhaustion overcame him and he lay down. Gracie curled herself against him, and he allowed himself to rest. He would change and pack a bag and get back to the hospital within the hour, but for that moment he allowed himself to sleep, with his therapy dog beside him.

CHAPTER SIXTEEN

THREE DAYS LATER, Susan was released from the hospital. Larry, Brooke, and Tara had taken turns staying with her during the day, but during a lucid moment on the second day of her hospitalization, Susan had insisted Larry sleep at their house with Gracie. Thankfully, Susan continued to improve, and when the results of her CT scans, blood work, and neurological assessments all came back clear, her doctors determined her well enough to be discharged— at which point the charge nurse came in and walked Larry through the care Susan would need over the next several weeks.

After helping her into the car, Larry nervously drove her home. He hadn't been this anxious behind the wheel since he'd driven his newborn daughters home decades ago.

"Is the air cool enough?" He turned the vent toward Susan. "Are you too cool?" He turned it away. He eased on the accelerator when the light turned green. "Is the ride too bumpy? Is your head hurting?"

He wanted to hear her tease him and say something snarky like *My head's only hurting because of your twenty questions*, but instead she just stared blankly out the windshield. Susan hadn't said much during her stay in the hospital. She was quiet, tentative, confused, and very, very tired. The doctors had sent her home with a prescription for Dilantin with strict orders to never let any doctor take her off of it. Between now and her follow-up appointment with the neurologist in two weeks, she was told to rest as much as possible. If Susan had any sign of bleeding or unrelieved pain, or if she started running a fever, Larry was instructed to call 911.

When they turned into their driveway and parked in the garage, Larry was struck by how different life had become in the four days since they'd returned home from vacation.

He hurried to Susan's door, opened it, put her arm around his shoulders, and half-carried her inside. She couldn't walk without help. Larry tried not to think too far ahead, but seeing Susan unable to hold herself up made it hard not to wonder about her prognosis. The doctor had said it would take time for the swelling in her brain to go down and for it to heal. But the what-ifs nagged Larry constantly.

At the door, Susan heard a deep bark from inside the house.

"Gra-cie," she mumbled.

Larry was encouraged. "Yep, that's our girl Gracie. She has missed you so much."

When Larry opened the door, Gracie's entire body wiggled and bounced with excitement. Larry knew his dog was ecstatic to see Susan, but he could feel his wife's body start to grow limp as she grew weaker from trying to stay upright.

"Easy, Grace," he instructed. "Let's get Susan to the sofa."

He slowly laid her on the end of the sectional and Gracie was immediately by her side, staring adoringly at her mom. Susan looked blankly at Gracie, then closed her eyes and fell asleep.

Larry sat down, leaned his head back, and once again pleaded with God for mercy and grace in healing Susan. He studied his wife's sleeping face, marred by a purple, yellow, and greenish-blue bruise across the right side of her face. The bruise encompassed her forehead, the tender skin under her eye, and her high cheekbone. Yet, even with her battered face, she was still beautiful. The most beautiful woman he had ever seen. He closed his eyes and allowed himself a moment's rest—a moment to remember the first time he laid eyes on her . . .

Ten years earlier, they were both working in commercial real estate. She was representing a shopping center developer and answered the phone when he called about a listing. She had a friendly voice and a quick wit and he enjoyed their conversations, but since he had a job to do, their conversations mainly centered on work. But several months later, Larry was at a real estate conference in Orlando when he spotted a beautiful woman with long blonde hair. He made his way across the small reception room and read her name tag.

"Are you the Susan I've been talking to on the phone a lot recently? I'm Larry Randolph."

Susan's cheeks had flushed as she smiled and nodded. They spent several minutes talking about their shared business ventures before Larry asked for her business card. "Could I set up a time to meet you for lunch?" he asked, feeling as nervous as a teenager asking a girl to prom.

Susan handed him her card. "I would enjoy that."

Five days later, Susan walked into Caffé Amaretto with a brief-case full of deals to discuss. Larry wasn't the least bit interested in the deals, but he was very interested in getting to know her.

"I had actually just gotten back into town the day before the conference from visiting my daughter and little grandson, Gib," Larry said as the server placed a basket of bread on their table. "He's three months old, and he already has me wrapped around his finger."

Susan's eyes brightened at the word *grandson*. She asked several questions about Gib and asked Larry what it was like to be a grandparent. She then shared about her young-adult daughters, the challenges of being a single mom, and the faith in God that saw her through a painful divorce. Larry was delighted to learn that they had three significant things in common: their faith, a deep love for their families, and a strong work ethic.

Larry asked for a second dinner date before they left the restaurant. "I know just where I'll take you," he said, beaming. Having grown up in New Orleans, Larry loved Cajun food and wanted to share that part of his history with the woman who was quickly becoming very important to him.

When the evening arrived for their second date, Susan asked Larry to order for her since she had never had Cajun food. Larry ordered crawfish étouffée—his favorite dish. Susan took one bite and her face turned beet red, her eyes watered, sweat beaded on her forehead, and she began gasping for breath.

"Here, drink some water," Larry said, holding her glass out to her, quickly followed by his.

"I didn't—" she nodded her thanks to the server who was refilling their glasses—"I didn't realize Cajun food was . . . so spicy."

Larry was worried she would want to leave, but instead she asked, "Do they have a kids' menu I could order from?"

Larry laughed, then motioned for the server, who assured Susan that the chicken fingers were not spicy at all. When her entrée arrived, the couple enjoyed the rest of their evening.

Larry chuckled at the memory. But when he opened his eyes and saw Susan's bruised and swollen face, the smile quickly vanished. *Father, please heal her brain, her face, and her spirit.* He touched her forehead and was grateful that it was cool. No fever. Larry gently laid a light blanket over her. As he sat back down on the sofa, Gracie jumped up beside him and rested her head on his lap. Larry watched Susan while stroking Gracie's head. Sweet memories warmed his heart.

Him and Susan meeting each other's children—nervous about how they would be received; delighted when both were welcomed with excitement and grace.

Proposing to Susan on Valentine's Day. How beautiful she looked when she said yes. How wonderful she felt in his arms as they dreamed about the future.

Eloping to Nantucket on the Fourth of July to avoid the stress and logistics of a large wedding for a blended family scattered all over the globe.

Their perfect wedding night.

Their first Christmas as a married couple.

Gracie jumped off the sofa. Her sudden movement jostled Larry and brought him back to the present. Gracie whimpered, signaling Larry to look at Susan.

"Susie, you're awake. Do you need anything?"

"Water," she whispered.

Larry hurried to the kitchen, returned with a glass, and held it for her as she drank. Susan looked around the room as if seeing it for the first time.

"I . . . need to . . ." her lips searched for words her brain couldn't find. "Bathroom."

Larry draped her arm around his shoulder and helped her walk to the bathroom. His breath caught as they crossed the threshold. *Give me strength, God*, he pleaded. After seeing to her needs, Larry got Susan resettled on the sofa.

A few minutes later, the doorbell rang. Friends from church were dropping off a meal.

"Here's dinner for tonight and some muffins for the morning."

Their thoughtfulness touched Larry deeply, the first of many friends who brought meals and groceries, who came to visit and pray, and who offered to clean and take Gracie for walks. Every time the doorbell rang, it was like God himself extending mercy and grace. Although Susan didn't say much those first three weeks after her accident, she smiled and became more animated every time the doorbell rang.

Thankfully, she became more mobile and less confused over time, too, eventually getting around with a walker. In the weeks right after the accident, Susan slurred and stumbled over her words. But eventually she was able to form complete sentences. Larry celebrated and thanked God for each and every milestone she reached.

Still, he struggled with the thought of leaving her alone for any amount of time—even just for a short walk with Gracie. He called all the places he routinely visited to let them know about Susan's accident and inform them he wouldn't be able to come for a while.

Ministry volunteers stepped in to cover his absence. He was thankful to God for providing a way to keep the ministry going without him, which made it possible for him to step back and focus on Susan. While she slept, Larry would return phone calls—both personal and those related to Canines for Christ, take Gracie for short walks, read his Bible, and pray. He also began talking with some trusted friends and counselors about the flashbacks, nightmares, and fears he was having since Susan's accident. They listened, prayed with him, and provided a safe place for him to process his anxiety, all of which helped minimize some of his symptoms.

❧

"I promise, I'll be fine," Susan said, seven weeks after her accident.

She was trying to convince Larry to visit the Trinity school. He had been to the school two times since her seizure when Brooke and Tara had stayed with Susan. Her friend Ellie was supposed to sit with her today, but she was running late, and Larry didn't want to leave her by herself.

"The doctor said I'm okay," Susan tried again. "And Ellie will be here now . . ." She scrunched her eyebrows and tried again. "She'll be here . . . soon," she corrected.

Gracie nudged Larry's hand and whined. She was wearing her red vest and ready to go. Larry wasn't. *What if Susan has another seizure? What if she falls again? What if she is alone when it happens?*

"I'll just call Terry and let her know I can't make it today."

Susan shook her head.

"They're waiting for you and Gracie. And they've planned a welcome back . . . party."

Gracie nosed his hand again.

"Okay, but I want you to stay on this sofa and not move until Ellie gets here."

Susan nodded and settled back against the cushions. Larry knew he was being led by his fear. The doctor was pleased with Susan's progress. She was regaining strength and mobility, even being able to go on short walks with him and Gracie around their neighborhood.

"Call me if you need anything. And I'll call you once I get there."

Twenty minutes later, Larry pulled into the Trinity parking lot and immediately dialed Susan's cell phone number. He breathed a sigh of relief when she answered and said Ellie had just arrived with lunch. Gracie jumped from the back seat and looked at Larry as if to ask, *Are you good now? Can we go to work?*

Larry enjoyed reconnecting with the Trinity students, and they were all thrilled to see and pet Gracie, whose tail didn't stop wagging during the hour-long visit. It was obvious that Gracie had missed working as a therapy dog. Suddenly it hit him: *Gracie had been acting as a therapy dog to Susan and him for the past six weeks.* "You've been working all along, haven't you, girl?" He reached his hand back and scratched her chin. "You really are my amazing Grace."

🐾

Four months after Susan's accident, life had returned to a new normal. She wasn't cleared to drive yet, but she was walking normally, running errands with Larry, able to hold her grandchildren, speaking clearly, and attending church services again. The only lingering effects of the head trauma were difficulty with complex tasks, remembering number sequences, and heightened anxiety. Susan had never struggled with anxiety before, but as her brain swelling decreased, anxiety symptoms increased. And with the anxiety came a short temper and emotional outbursts—something she had never struggled with before.

Laura proved to be a valuable resource for Larry and Susan as she had experienced similar symptoms following her accident and traumatic brain injury. Once again Larry marveled at God's provision—not only had the ministry provided direction and purpose for Laura, she had become a helpful resource to their family.

And now, Laura and Chloe were joining him at Trinity for a weekly Bible study he had started three weeks earlier. Terry had loved the idea when Larry had mentioned it just before Susan's seizure. He had put it on hold after her accident, but as she began to heal, Larry found himself thinking about it again and reached out to Terry. Larry had been thrilled when nine people showed up for the first meeting. He welcomed everyone, walked Gracie around, and spent fifteen minutes talking to them about the meaning of John 3:16—about how much God loves them and how special they are to him. He ended by taking prayer requests and praying for each one.

The feedback from the first Bible study meeting was so positive that Larry hadn't been surprised when twelve people came the next week. Or when fifteen participated the next.

He wondered how many would be there today. But then he quickly reminded himself that his job was to simply show up and let God love people through him, and through Gracie—the results of his obedience were up to God. *You bring them, Lord, and I'll do my best to show them your love*, he resolved.

"How is Susan today?" Laura asked Larry.

"She was playing with her granddaughters when I left," he reported with a smile.

Laura was excited to tell him about her recent visit with Chloe to a nursing home and how the Lab had ministered to a woman with dementia. Laura also informed him that she would be going back into the hospital to have a surgical procedure done on her back. She was still experiencing a great deal of pain and was hopeful this latest procedure would help. Larry listened intently and made a mental note to pray for her the day of her procedure, but as he listened, he also found himself wondering if, or when, he might have to undergo surgery himself. He was on his third cortisone shot, and his ankle pain was only getting worse. His doctor said surgery was the only option going forward, but Larry wasn't quite ready for that yet. He was hopeful that another doctor might have a less invasive treatment. He led his small team in prayer, asking God to pour out his loving-kindness through them, and committed their Bible study time to him.

"Everyone ready?" he asked.

"Ready," Laura answered.

Gracie and Chloe answered with wagging tails and excited panting.

"Then let's go to work."

"Dogs are here!" A middle-aged man named Richard heralded their arrival as Larry and Laura entered Trinity with their dogs. The friendly man adored Gracie, and when Cody retired he declared Gracie to be their new wonder dog.

"Dogs!" several other voices called out as the group walked down the hallway. Heads poked out of classrooms and arms waved greetings.

"Chaplain Larry brought a new dog and a new person!" a woman named Emmeline announced.

Larry led Gracie and the others into the first classroom on the right where they would be meeting for Bible study.

"There's two Gracies," a jovial man named Dennis observed.

"The dogs do look alike, don't they?" Larry chuckled. "Chloe is a white Labrador Retriever like Gracie. She belongs to Laura and her husband, Carl."

"Chloe and I are so glad to be here," Laura said.

Larry sensed that she felt a bit uncomfortable being surrounded by fifteen pairs of eager hands and excited voices. But she smiled warmly as she interacted with those in attendance, and Larry had no doubt she would fall in love with Trinity as much as he had. Larry invited everyone to sit wherever they were most comfortable. Some sat on the floor with the dogs, others sat at tables, and a few pulled their chairs near the dogs. When everyone had found a place, Larry opened with prayer.

"Heavenly Father, we know that you are here with us. Your love is here, and it shines in the hearts of these special people. Thank you for loving us. And thank you for giving us your words in the Bible. Please talk and teach through me today, and please let my friends here know how special they are to you and how much you love them."

"Amen!" a chorus of voices shouted.

Larry pulled out his Bible and opened it to John 15. He asked the group if they had a best friend. Several shouted out the name of their best friend; two named Gracie as their best friend; and a few others said they didn't have a best friend.

"Actually, you all have a very special best friend," Larry told them.

"I don't," Emmeline said, frowning.

"I'm going to read some words from the Bible—some things that Jesus said, and when I'm done, I want you to tell me what Jesus calls you, okay?"

"Okay," she said. She leaned forward and closed her eyes to listen.

Larry read, "I no longer call you servants, because a servant does not know his master's business. Instead, I have called you friends, for everything that I learned from my Father I have made known to you" (John 15:15).

He looked at Emmeline. "What did Jesus call you? He said he doesn't call us servants. Instead, he calls us what?"

She smiled shyly. "His friend."

"That's right. Jesus came to earth to show us God's love and to be our friend. He loves us so much that he left heaven and lived among people. That means he knows how it feels to be cold and tired and sore. He felt pain and he felt lonely. He also did miracles."

Larry asked if anyone could name one of Jesus' miracles. The answers came quickly—feeding a large group of people from one small lunch, walking on water, and healing people.

"And the greatest miracle Jesus did was dying on a cross and then coming back to life so that we can live with him forever—and so we can be his friends."

"Jesus is my friend," Richard declared.

"He's my friend too," Emmeline answered.

As each one in the group declared Jesus as their friend, Larry proudly watched Gracie and Chloe interact with them individually.

"Before we go, does anyone have a prayer request?" Larry asked. "A prayer request is a problem or worry that you want to tell your friend Jesus about." Every hand went up.

Laura took out a notebook and began writing down the requests. Several students asked for prayer for family members who were sick. Richard asked for prayer to see his mom soon. He lived in a facility and hadn't seen her for several weeks. Emmeline said she missed her sister who died a few years ago. Then Willie, a man in a wheelchair, slowly lifted his arm. He had been there the last two times, but he hadn't said anything. Larry smiled at him and asked how they could pray for him.

"I want to find my family. Will you ask my friend Jesus to help me find them?"

Larry smiled even as his heart broke at the soft-spoken man's request. He thanked him for sharing and assured him he would pray. After praying over every request, Larry and Laura gave the students goodbye hugs. On the way out of the school, they stopped to ask Terry about Willie's family.

"He's been in and out of special-needs group homes and facilities most of his life. And as far as I know, he doesn't have any family. Or if he does, they haven't made any effort to find him."

Larry heard Laura inhale deeply. He knew her heart was breaking for Willie as much as his own was. After debriefing in the parking lot, Laura asked if she and Chloe could return the following week.

"I wasn't sure this was a good fit for us at first, but I loved it so much. I want to be a part of this place and these people. Thank you for inviting me today."

CHAPTER SEVENTEEN

ON THE DRIVE HOME FROM TRINITY, Larry reflected on all God was doing through the ministry as he listened to his favorite worship song on the radio. Things were finally feeling normal again, and he was ready to get back to full-time ministry. He pulled into the garage, excited to tell Susan about the Bible study. He opened the back door for Gracie, and she jumped out like she always did. But instead of heading to the door, she stood still and looked at him.

"Come on, girl," he said, wondering why she was hesitating.

A moment later he knew why she hesitated—she was limping. Inside the house, he walked her to the large rug in the middle of the family room, had her lie down, and began examining her legs.

"What's the matter?" Susan asked.

"She's limping. I think she might have stepped on something in the Trinity parking lot."

Larry felt each paw. There were no pebbles or slivers of wood stuck between her toes. Her nails looked fine. He couldn't find any cuts or sores on the pads of her paws. When he ran his hands over each leg, she didn't whimper or yelp. But when she walked to her water bowl, she had a noticeable limp. He skipped their evening walk and sat on the floor with her that evening so she didn't try to jump up on the sofa. He hoped a night of rest would help, but when she was still limping the next morning, he called the vet clinic for an appointment that day.

"Brief periods of limping are common in large breeds," the vet said as he examined Gracie's front right leg—the one he had determined to be the source of her discomfort. "She likely twisted it or overextended it. Let's try some anti-inflammatory pills and have her rest for a few days. I imagine it will resolve itself. If not, we can do some more tests to see what else might be going on."

Back home, getting Gracie to rest proved difficult. She didn't seem to understand why she needed to stay off her legs. She wanted to patrol her yard for golf balls, her pool for frogs, and the front window for the mail carrier. Out of desperation to get his dog to lie down and stay down, Larry lay in the closet with her, next to her bed. After a few minutes of staring at him with a confused and curious look, Gracie finally laid her head down and rested for several hours. Larry quietly slipped out of the closet and got to his feet, limping as well from being cramped in an awkward position. After three days of rest and medicine, Gracie seemed to be doing better. She limped slightly when she first got up in the morning, but she was fine after she moved around a bit.

"Do you think Gracie can go to the courthouse tomorrow?" Susan asked over breakfast.

Two days earlier, Larry had been ready to ask another Canines for Christ volunteer to cover his prescheduled visit to the court-house. But something in his gut had told him to wait. And now as he watched his dog walk with ease, he believed his gut had been right.

"I do," Larry said. "As long as she doesn't start limping today, I think the visit will do her good. And I get the feeling she wants to get back to work."

The moment the words left his mouth, he realized his mistake. Gracie ran to her vest hanging on the wall. She wagged her tail and panted her readiness. "Sorry, girl, not yet. Tomorrow."

When Gracie stood by her vest with her tail beating against the wall, Larry got a cup of her special Frosty Paws ice cream out of the freezer. If he couldn't make her understand, he could at least redirect her focus. Thankfully, the icy treat did just that.

The next morning Gracie could barely contain her excitement as Larry clipped on her vest. Larry loved seeing his dog so happy, and yet his spirit was heavy, knowing why they were going to the court-house today. A few weeks earlier, a counselor with a local crisis and trauma center had contacted him, requesting a therapy dog for a young client who had been sexually abused. The ten-year-old girl was set to testify in court and was becoming more fearful as the court date approached. Having heard about the benefits of therapy dogs working with abuse survivors, the counselor had discovered Canines for Christ and called to see if they could make a dog available to the brave girl. Larry hadn't hesitated. "I will be there myself with my beautiful dog, Gracie," he had told her.

The trauma counselor was waiting for him outside the court-house when he walked up with Gracie.

"You must be Larry and Gracie," she said, extending her hand.

"I'm Amanda. I'll take you inside to meet Charley and her grand-mother, Patty. Charley is very scared today—which is understandable. I think seeing Gracie will help a lot."

Larry took a deep breath. *Charlie.* A pang of grief hit as he thought of his friend from the VA. He prayed that the little girl would prove to be as tough and resilient as the old veteran who shared her name. Larry followed Amanda through the security check and into a small room off the main lobby. A little girl with shoulder-length brown hair and thick bangs sat next to a woman with glasses. The little girl's eyes had a faraway look that made Larry's chest ache. She started to turn away from him, but then Gracie appeared from behind his legs and Charley stood up. She walked to Gracie, sat on the floor, and wrapped her thin arms around the dog.

"Charley, this is Gracie and her friend Chaplain Larry," Amanda said. "They are here for you. *Just* for you. They aren't here for the lawyers, the judge, or anyone else in the courtroom. Only you. Their whole job today is to help you feel a little less scared."

Larry appreciated the way the counselor explained his role. And by the way Charley's eyes brightened and she sat up a little straighter, Larry sensed the little girl appreciated it too. Larry asked Gracie to sit and asked Charley if she wanted to shake Gracie's hand. She nodded, then giggled when Gracie placed her right front paw on her hand.

"What else can she do?"

Larry showed Charley how Gracie could roll over, sit, stand, show her belly, and do Paws Up on a table.

"She's smart."

Father, only you can bring joy to a little girl's heart as she prepares to face her abuser, Larry prayed in awe of the way God was ministering to this young girl through Gracie.

"She *is* smart," Larry agreed, "and she's brave too."

Larry gave Charley an abbreviated version of how Gracie had alerted him to Susan's seizure, and how she visited people in noisy places like hospitals and schools—places that often scared other dogs. Charley listened intently to Larry while running her hand up and down Gracie's back.

"Gracie can sense that you're smart and brave too."

"She thinks I'm brave?"

"I bet Gracie thinks you're one of the bravest girls she knows. What you're doing today is very brave."

Charley's gaze fell to the floor. "But I'm scared."

Oh, how his heart ached for this girl. Gracie scooted closer to her.

"It's okay to feel scared. What you're doing today is very scary. Gracie is the bravest dog I know, and she gets scared sometimes too. But Gracie taught me something important about being scared. Would you like to know what she taught me?"

Charley nodded.

"Scared is where courage grows. If we never felt scared, we'd never learn to have courage."

"*Gracie* taught you that?" Charley asked skeptically.

"Well . . . she helps me remember it. I actually learned that from one of the bravest men I've ever known. I bet you'll never guess his name."

Her pale blue eyes sparkled with curiosity.

"Um, George?"

"Good guess. But his name was . . . Charlie."

"Really?" The girl's smile brightened the room.

"Really," Larry confirmed. "Charlie fought in a war. He got injured and had to have a lot of surgeries, and he was often in a lot of pain, but he never let the darkness win. He got sad and mad, and sometimes he got scared, but he always tried to find something good in his days. And do you know what one of his favorite good things was?"

"What?" the girl asked, her fingers massaging Gracie's ears.

"Seeing Gracie. He loved petting her. And he said Gracie helped him feel brave."

Charley studied Gracie for several silent minutes. And as she did, Larry prayed.

"They're ready for Charley," Amanda announced. She crouched down in front of her. "Remember: You are safe. He can't touch you. He can't talk to you. All you need to do is answer some questions and you'll be done. And you can look at Gracie the whole time you're in there, okay?"

The little girl clung to Gracie, and Gracie rested her head on Charley's shoulder.

Father, give her strength. Surround her with your angels. Speak through her and to her, Larry prayed.

"Gracie will come with me, right?" she asked, her bottom lip quivering.

Larry handed Gracie's leash to Charley.

"Gracie won't leave your side."

Charley took Gracie's leash, put her shoulders back, and walked into the courtroom. When she took the witness stand, Gracie positioned herself right in front of Charley, facing her. The brave girl never took her eyes off the dog. After she was done, Charley was trembling and threw her arms around Gracie in the hallway, allowing the tears she had been holding back to stream down her cheeks. Larry asked if he could pray with Charley and her grandmother. Afterward he handed Charley a pocket-sized wooden cross.

"Whenever you hold this, I hope you will remember Gracie, and how brave you were, and most important, I hope you will think about how much God loves you and that he's always with you."

On the way home Larry continued to pray for the brave young girl and marveled at all that had just transpired. Pastor Matthew's words from years ago had proved true today. Jesus entered the courthouse "wrapped in fur," the coat of a white Lab named Gracie.

Over the next six weeks, Gracie made several visits to the VA hospital, Trinity, Suncoast, and some local hospitals and nursing homes. She seemed thrilled to be back to work, but it came at a cost. By the end of each evening, she would begin limping again. They went to the vet again for X-rays and blood work. Larry anxiously awaited the results, fearing his beloved dog might have cancer. Memories of Gus rushed through his mind at night. *Please, Lord, don't let me lose her. She's your dog. She's doing your work. Please let her live a long and healthy life.*

When the vet confirmed that there was no evidence of cancer, Larry was relieved. Yet, the X-rays revealed no additional information. Larry scaled back Gracie's visits, hoping that less time on her feet would help. Unfortunately, the limp only worsened. Larry and Susan decided to get a second opinion and took Gracie to a different vet.

"I think we're looking at a ligament issue" was the diagnosis.

He recommended hydrotherapy, which involved Gracie swimming and walking in a whirlpool bath while the warm water massaged her joints. Gracie seemed to enjoy the treatments, and they did seem to help somewhat, but a few weeks after the treatment ended, she was limping again. She wasn't the only one. Larry's ankle pain was worsening as well. He began icing his ankle every night. He knew he would need to address his own pain soon enough, but he was far too focused on Gracie to worry about that now.

When Gracie's limping became more pronounced throughout the day, Larry made the difficult decision to limit her visits to one a week—Trinity's Bible study. Larry believed it was important to maintain consistency for the students. And he knew that they, perhaps more than most, would understand and accommodate Gracie's limitations. He was right. The students were sympathetic to her injury and even made a blanket for her to lie on during their visits.

"We will come to you, Gracie," Richard said. "You don't have to walk to us."

Their kindness touched Larry deeply. As he watched the group of thirty-five people surround his dog and love on her, he realized they were grateful for the opportunity to care for her, just as she had been caring for them.

A month passed, and once again Larry and Susan were taking Gracie to a new vet for a third opinion, hoping for a fresh perspective and treatment plan.

"After looking at the images we took," Dr. Evans began, "I believe Gracie has some tearing in her ligament which could lead to significant arthritis if it isn't repaired. I would recommend arthroscopy to evaluate the joint and, if needed, make the necessary repair."

It was a quiet ride home as they processed the information.

Gracie limped to her favorite spot in front of the sliding glass doors.

"What do you think?" Susan asked, handing Larry a glass of iced tea.

He took a long sip and leaned back in his recliner. "I will do whatever it takes to get her feeling better. I'd take the pain from her if God would let me. But I just don't know about surgery—at least not yet. What do you think?"

"I agree. I don't have peace about the surgery. But maybe it's too soon for us to make this decision. Why don't we take a few days and pray about it?"

"That sounds good," Larry agreed. "We're already on our third opinion, so maybe we should get one more?"

"That's true—and who knows, maybe for us it will be the *fourth* time that's the charm," Susan joked.

Larry chuckled. It was so good to have his wife—and her sense of humor—back.

🐾

A week later, after spending a lot of time in prayer and talking to friends whose dogs had faced similar issues, Larry and Susan were still feeling uneasy about scheduling surgery for Gracie. They contacted a veterinarian who came highly recommended by a Canines for Christ volunteer. "God, please make your will clear to us," Larry prayed as they drove to yet another clinic. "We ask that you heal Gracie and continue to work through her to bring your love to many people."

"I agree that surgery may be necessary," Dr. Burroughs said.

Larry's heart dropped—maybe it was God's will for Gracie to undergo surgery.

"But I would like to try laser treatments first."

Larry's heart soared.

"Laser treatments?"

Dr. Burroughs explained the procedure. They would use a cold laser to concentrate a specific form of light to the area causing Gracie's pain.

"The goal would be for the cold laser therapy to stimulate her tissue cells to grow and repair the damaged tissue. It's painless, although it often takes several treatments before we notice improvement. And sometimes it doesn't give us the outcome we'd like, and we end up proceeding with a surgical option."

Larry appreciated Dr. Burroughs's honesty—and having another option. They wasted no time scheduling Gracie's treatments. She would undergo cold laser therapy once a week for eight weeks and only go once a week to Trinity's Bible study.

🐾

Three days after her first laser treatment, Gracie was lying at Larry's feet as he spent time in God's Word and in prayer. "Gracie's your dog, Lord. Please heal her and allow her to serve you for many years. It's been hard to scale back on visits. We both miss it. Please continue to bless the ministry and do good work through our volunteers."

After finishing his quiet time, he opened his email. He replied to several requests for more information about the ministry, deleted a half dozen spam emails, then clicked on a message with the subject line "Thank You."

Hello. Not too long ago, I had been fighting for my life from an unknown illness. I was so discouraged.

So tired. And I didn't know if I could go on. But then I met Canines for Christ volunteers Amy and Bo and the greatest dog in the whole wide world, Rafa. They laid Rafa on my bed, and my heart melted. My mom told them what was going on with me. I couldn't believe it when Amy said that Rafa had been rescued after fighting for his life and almost dying. And for the first time, I felt like I could get through my illness. I saw it as temporary. I could fight like Rafa, and the doctors would find a way to help me so I could get back to life again. And I did. THANK YOU for starting this wonderful ministry. You, your amazing dogs, and the caring people who pray and talk with people during some of the most difficult parts of our lives really make a difference. I'm still feeling the happiness, hope, and joy from being lucky enough to have seen Rafa and Amy and Bo. You all are giving people hope, even when circumstances seem impossible. We appreciate you. We need you. I am so thankful for this organization and all the amazing owners and therapy dogs that are changing lives for the better every day.

A. Ricca

Larry sat back in his chair. *Wow.* "Father, I was not expecting that. Thank you for touching that young person's life through Rafa and our volunteers."

He had so much more to say, to praise God for, and yet all he could do was sit in stunned silence and marvel at God's provision—to expand the reach and impact of the ministry at the same time Larry and Gracie were having to step back from visits. "It's like watching you feed thousands of people from a few loaves and some fish."

🐾

"I know, girl," Larry tried to explain to Gracie as they headed to her sixth cold laser treatment. "I know you want your vest on, but we have to get you better first."

Gracie's tail wagged, hoping Larry would grab her red vest, and her head dropped in disappointment when it remained on the hook. The almost-four-year-old Lab loved spending time with her friends at Trinity, but it was clear she missed going other places. Her limp had improved somewhat, but not as much as Larry had hoped. Her pain seemed less, but it was still evident. Larry feared they would soon be looking at surgery. After finishing the treatment, Dr. Burroughs met with them.

"I'm happy with the progress she's making, but we're not where I'd like her to be."

Larry braced himself for what he knew was coming. He was so busy thinking several steps ahead—how long her recovery would last and how to tell the Trinity students that she couldn't visit for a while—that he almost missed the vet's next words.

"So if you're okay with it, I'd like to do another round of laser treatments. I really think this is the best way to go and that she will respond well. I think she just needs a little more time."

Larry wanted to hug the man. A little more time sounded great to him.

And it turned out that a little more time was exactly what Gracie needed because after the twelfth treatment, Dr. Burroughs declared her well enough to avoid surgery. Gracie would take a daily joint-health supplement and receive a monthly steroid injection for a while, but with her limp gone and no evidence of any pain, she could resume her normal schedule. Larry was ecstatic. He was anxious to let his dog get back to the work they both loved.

It was good to be back at the VA hospital. Larry had missed the regular patients and staff, and he was delighted to meet new ones. On Gracie's first day back, he kept their visit to one wing of the sprawling campus. He didn't want her to overdo it. They also made a quick stop at a nursing home and then visited with a man from their church who had recently been admitted to St. Joseph's Hospital. A flood of painful memories rushed through Larry's heart as he entered the hospital where Susan had been taken almost a year earlier. Gracie, seeming to sense his mood, slowed her steps and pressed her body next to him, a tangible reminder of God's faithfulness through the highs and lows of his life. He rubbed her head. "Thanks, girl."

Later that night, after feeding Gracie and then retrieving a golf ball from her mouth and a frog from the pool, Larry walked to his favorite spot on the sofa. He had earned some ESPN time. But when he pivoted to grab the remote before sitting down, pain shot through his ankle, and he fell onto the sofa. The pain was so intense, he became nauseous. When a large dose of ibuprofen and constant ice could only make the pain tolerable, Larry knew that, unlike his dog, he was no longer able to put off surgery.

CHAPTER EIGHTEEN

"You need to keep your ankle elevated at all times to minimize
swelling," the surgeon said, reviewing Larry's post-op instructions
two days after his total ankle replacement. "You will be in this soft
cast for two weeks, then we will put you in a hard cast for three
months. During this time, you should not bear any weight on
your ankle. And no showers or baths—only sponge bathing until
the soft cast comes off." He flipped through the chart in his hand.
"I see that they've already set you up with a wheelchair. As your
healing progresses, you will be able to transition to a knee scooter
or a walker."

Larry nodded but found it hard to fully absorb what the doctor
was saying. He was still a little fuzzy from the pain medication.
Thankfully, Susan was there and would help him remember the
instructions. A nurse handed her a stack of papers, with all his

post-op instructions, follow-up appointments, and prescriptions for pain medication and an antibiotic.

"Ready to go?" the nurse asked after the doctor left.

Larry was very ready. He was ready to sleep in his own bed, eat his own food, and be reunited with Gracie.

When he and Susan arrived home, Larry struggled to get out of the SUV and into the wheelchair he would be using for the next three months. Susan pushed the chair right up next to his car door and tried to help steady him as he maneuvered himself from the passenger seat to the chair. It took several attempts, and was an awkward transfer, but he eventually made it. Susan pushed him up the temporary plywood ramp leading from the garage into the house.

It's going to be a long three months, Larry thought.

But the moment he saw Gracie, his thoughts turned to his excited dog and the happy sounds she was making. Gracie barked and whined, grunted and moaned. She licked his hands, then laid her head on his lap. Susan shielded Larry's right ankle so their exuberant dog didn't bump it.

"Oh, I missed you, Gracie," Larry said. "And I hope you missed me, because we're going to be spending a lot of time together over the next few months."

Gracie's soulful eyes gazed into Larry's. Then she spontaneously did Paws Up and kissed his face.

Gracie quickly stepped into the role of therapy dog for Larry. During the first two weeks of his recovery, aside from the brief times Susan took Gracie outside to do her business or for a short walk, Gracie was by his side. She lay next to him on the sofa while he watched TV, sat next to him during meals, and kept watch over him as he napped. Larry had canceled all of his Canines for

Christ visits for the duration of his recovery but was hopeful he and Gracie would be able to go to Trinity once he got used to the hard cast. He would still be in the wheelchair, but since it was a small campus designed to accommodate wheelchairs, he would be perfectly able to navigate it. Thankfully, Laura and Chloe and a few other volunteer teams were covering the weekly Bible study group until he was able to return.

The first few weeks of his recovery were fine. He and Susan spent a lot of time together watching TV, discussing future plans, and going over ministry business, which had slowed down. Larry had noticed the same decrease both in volunteer interest and requests for visits during Susan's recovery. Since the two of them managed all of the ministry's administrative tasks, he saw less activity as a blessing and God's provision for them. But by the fourth week, Larry was bored and grumpy.

"I am so tired of seeing these same walls," he complained to Susan.

He could have sworn she mumbled something about being tired of seeing him, but he didn't want to ask her to repeat or confirm.

"Why don't I take you and Gracie to the mall? I think the change of scenery would do both of you good."

Larry was a little nervous at the thought of leaving the house, but his excitement outweighed his fear, and an hour later, the three of them were in the food court at the mall. After finishing lunch, Susan left Larry and Gracie on their own while she ran errands.

"I'll be back at two o'clock." She gave him a quick kiss, then patted Gracie's head. "You're in charge, Gracie. Take care of him."

Larry looped Gracie's leash around his arm and started maneuvering his chair down the mall concourse. Gracie had become proficient at walking beside him as he steered his wheelchair. She had learned to slow her pace to match his, and she never pulled on the leash. Larry was excited to interact with others there, but aside from a few people glancing and smiling at Gracie, no one paid attention to him. When he tried to initiate a conversation, more often than not, he was met with awkward silence or dismissive smiles.

Later that night, after enjoying a nice dinner with Susan and a beautiful sunset by the pool, Larry decided that he had likely been overly sensitive at the mall. *I was probably just feeling self-conscious.*

But five days later, when he returned to the mall with Gracie, the same thing happened.

"It was like I was invisible—even with Gracie beside me," he explained to Susan on the way home. "Some people would look at Gracie but then quickly turn away from me. And others ignored us completely—wouldn't even look at me. I don't know if they just didn't know what to say or maybe my being in a wheelchair made them feel uncomfortable. But the whole time I was there I kept thinking about our Trinity friends and how what I experienced today is likely a fraction of what they have experienced their entire lives."

The experience increased Larry's resolve to get back to Trinity as soon as possible. He felt a renewed passion for making sure those men and women knew that they were adored and seen by God, and by himself and Gracie.

A few days later, a woman named Jane called him. She had written a Bible study featuring stories of her dogs, specifically geared for adults with developmental disabilities.

"I came across your website while researching ministries and churches that might have a need for a resource like this," she said after introducing herself. "I'd love to meet with you and give you a copy of the book. It's based on my two dogs, Zeke and Jimmy, and all the adventures they get themselves into."

A Bible study about two dogs for adults with developmental challenges? It sounded perfect for what he was doing at Trinity. Larry admired Jane's passion and initiative, and he immediately said yes.

"Wonderful!" she exclaimed. "I can be there next Friday. And I'll bring Jimmy with me. He's a little stinker—you'll see that in the book. But the little stinker loves road trips, so he'll enjoy driving to Florida with me."

"Oh, I thought you were local," Larry confessed. "Where are you coming from?"

"Minnesota."

Larry was glad he hadn't just taken a drink of his tea. *Minnesota!* He didn't think he'd ever set up a meeting with someone who would be traveling such a distance. They finalized the details for Jane's visit, which included her reading a story from her book to the Trinity Bible study group.

Over lunch, Larry filled Susan in on Jane's phone call and upcoming visit. Then she drove him and Gracie to Trinity for a prearranged short visit. When Susan pushed him through the door, his breath caught in his chest. A giant sign stretched across the wall in the lobby.

WELCOME BACK, PASTOR LARRY!

"Oh, Larry," Susan said with tears in her eyes.

Forty people were in the large multipurpose room, and they erupted in cheers and applause when the three came through the door. Larry had tears in his eyes too.

"Pastor Larry's in a chair like me!" Willie said.

"Like my chair too!" Thomas chimed in.

"Me too!" several other voices echoed.

"We made you a cake!" Emmeline said, tapping his shoulder repeatedly. "It's chocolate and really good. I tasted it."

Larry had come to encourage them, but they were the ones blessing him.

"I am so glad to see each and every one of you," he said. "And I pray that you all feel as loved and special as you have made me feel. Gracie and I have missed you so much."

"We made Gracie a doggie cake!" a woman named Jackie said, as Ed held a cupcake-sized treat out for her.

Gracie devoured it in two bites, to everyone's delight. Larry anticipated doing his usual round of classroom visits and then a brief prayer time but when Willie shouted, "Can we have Bible time now?" Larry jumped on the idea.

Taking a cue from the exuberant mood in the room, he led everyone in singing, "I've Got the Joy" and "This Is the Day." The joyful noise they made touched Larry's heart, and he knew it touched God's even more. Larry talked to them about Jesus and how he spent his time on earth seeing people—all people, even people whom no one else saw. "Jesus wasn't afraid to touch people with skin diseases, to talk to people others wouldn't talk to, to spend time with people others ignored.

"Jesus loves people," Larry said. "He loves all people. He loves you. No matter how you feel about yourself or how you think others feel about you, I want you to hear me—Jesus loves you."

He led them in singing "Jesus Loves Me." And then Willie requested "Amazing Grace." Larry didn't know if a song had ever sounded more beautiful—especially when Gracie began barking and howling toward the end of the song.

"Gracie's singing!" Thomas shouted.

Larry chuckled and assumed she had just gotten caught up in

the excitement, but when they sang a second verse and she began howling again, he couldn't deny the fact that Gracie did seem to be singing along—to what she probably thought was a song about her.

"I like dog church," Willie commented as Larry, Susan, and Gracie were saying their goodbyes.

Dog Church.

The phrase hit Larry's heart like a freight train. Dog Church! A church for those who are unable to participate in a traditional church service. Larry knew that most of the people at Trinity did not attend a church because of their physical limitations and developmental and emotional challenges. In that moment, he resolved to change that. From now on, Bible study time would become Dog Church, and anyone who wanted to participate was welcome. It might not be a traditional church service in a traditional church building. *But our church will have something no other church has*, Larry thought, glancing at Gracie. *Our church will have a singing dog.*

🐾

Two days after the idea for Dog Church was born, Larry received a call from Laura, asking for Gracie's breeder's name.

"Carl wants to start volunteering with me," she said excitedly. "And since Chloe is getting older and needing to slow down, we thought it would be a good time to get another dog. We absolutely love Gracie, so we thought we'd contact the same breeder to see if she has any available puppies."

Larry gladly gave her Denise's number. Twenty minutes later a much more subdued Laura called. "Denise doesn't have any puppies right now, and the next two litters are already spoken for. I told her about Canines for Christ and that we want to get a dog like Gracie. She took our information and said she would let us know when their next litter is planned."

Larry spent several minutes on the phone with Laura before ending their time in prayer and asking God to provide the right dog in his perfect timing. Four days later . . .

"Larry!" Laura squealed into the phone, "Denise just called. She has a dog for us! Someone returned a dog to her. They had used the dog for breeding and then decided they were done with her. Can you imagine?" Larry could not.

"Anyway, she's a *four*-year-old white English Lab." Her words hung in the air, as if she was waiting for him to deduce something from them. "Larry, the dog that was returned to Denise is from the same litter as Gracie. She is Gracie's sister!"

Larry couldn't believe it. *Only God.*

Laura and Carl picked up the dog the very next day and named her Leah. After a few days, Laura called Larry and asked if they could bring Leah over for a dog sister reunion. Larry didn't know how the two dogs would respond to each other. *Would they remember each other?* By the way they jumped on each other, wagged their tails, and romped around, he suspected they did. Leah seemed as gentle and loving as Gracie, and he had no doubt she would make an excellent ambassador for the ministry.

🐾

The following Friday, Larry met Jane and her terrier, Jimmy, outside Trinity. "Hi, Jane! It's so nice to meet you. Please forgive me for not getting up," Larry joked, patting his wheelchair and telling her about his ankle replacement.

Gracie sniffed Jimmy, then sat beside Larry while he and Jane talked about her work, the book, and the idea for Dog Church.

"That is absolutely wonderful!" Jane said. "I just love how you are giving them a place where they are free to worship and express themselves—and *be* themselves. If my little book can help in any way, I will feel so honored to be a small part of that."

Larry flipped through the pages, skimming the collection of short stories that anyone could read and lead a group through. And he loved that the stories were based on dogs. He introduced Jane to Terry when they entered the building, and then Larry led the way to the large room reserved for a special Friday edition of Dog Church. Forty-two people were waiting and many of the students fussed over Jimmy. After the group sang a few songs, Jane read them a story from *Adventures of Zeke and Jimmy*. Every time she read Jimmy's name, fingers around the room pointed in his direction. The students listened closely, and several people even answered the simple questions she asked at the end of the story. When she finished, Larry asked for prayer requests, and he and Jane prayed over each one.

"That was absolutely wonderful," Jane said on the way out. "I can't remember the last time church felt that much like . . . well, like what I imagine God intended church to be."

Larry couldn't have agreed more.

🐾

Three months after Larry's surgery, he had the hard cast removed and was learning how to walk in an orthopedic boot. He was glad to be able to move around a little more, but walking in the boot was awkward and painful. And he was still far from being able to drive. He would have to wait another month or two before his right ankle was strong enough to maneuver the pedals.

"I feel bad that you will have to keep driving Gracie and me to all of our visits," he said to Susan on the drive home from his doctor's visit.

Susan gave him the same look he saw her give little Luke the week before when he wanted to eat all the cookies—right out of the oven.

"Larry, you're in an orthopedic boot, not a magic boot. It's going to take you a while to get back to your usual schedule of visits. Take it from me—it's going to take longer than you think it should. But I'm here for you just like you were there for me. We will get you through this."

He knew she was right, but he was growing impatient with just how long it was taking. And if he was being completely honest, Larry was getting a little worried at his long-term prognosis. The surgeon had said this wasn't a permanent fix and that some patients required additional surgeries and procedures. *What if I will never be able to return to a normal schedule of visits?* He shook the thought away. *At least I have Trinity.*

Gracie met him at the door with a tennis ball in her mouth. Her tail thumped against the wall as she barked her muffled delight. Larry took her outside and let her run off some energy while he returned several calls he had missed—two from volunteers checking on him and sharing stories from recent experiences and another one from a member of their church small group who had received a cancer diagnosis and was asking for prayer. The last three missed calls were from prospective volunteers wanting to learn more about the ministry—and two of the three were from people who lived out of state. They had learned about the ministry from an online search for therapy dog organizations.

"God, this has always been, and will always be, your ministry," he prayed aloud that evening while Gracie patrolled the pool deck for frogs. "Thank you for keeping things at a slower pace while Susan, Gracie, and I have been recovering." He marveled again over the truth of that statement. Interests and activities were starting to pick up again, and he was sensing that they were going to pick up quickly. "Father, I don't know how much I am going to be able to do over the next few months, but I know that you will provide. Please continue to bring people into the ministry who will spread your message of love and help us continue to be what you want us to be."

CHAPTER NINETEEN

Larry pulled into the VA hospital's parking lot, grateful to be back. He unloaded Gracie from the back seat and walked her to a grassy area. The air was humid and the lingering summer heat made beads of sweat form on Larry's forehead. The calendar indicated October, but the weather felt more like August.

Canines for Christ had transitioned from being a small church-affiliated ministry to a full-fledged 501(c)(3) nonprofit. This change was necessary because the ministry had grown to more than three hundred volunteers—many of whom lived out of state. Susan took care of all the administrative tasks, and Larry handled the ministry inquiries and training of all the volunteers.

"All right, girl," Larry said, "let's go to work."

They started their day in the main hospital, visiting newly

admitted patients and their families. As they were passing one of the nurses' stations, a voice said, "It's my favorite canine superhero!"

A nurse named Linda came around the partition, squatted down, and opened her arms wide, inviting Gracie in. Larry referred to Linda as the energizer bunny. However, she seemed less peppy than usual. Larry started to ask if he could pray for her, but before he got a word out, she sat on the floor behind the nurse's station, pulled Gracie gently onto her lap, and put her head on the retriever. Larry silently prayed for Linda, knowing she carried burdens and cared for those who carried burdens. He asked God to give her strength and peace as well as an awareness of his love for her. Several minutes later, Linda planted a noisy kiss on the top of Gracie's head and rose to her feet.

"Thank you, Super Gracie, I really needed that." She patted Larry's arm as she walked by, heading down the hallway.

"All right, Super Gracie, let's catch the elevator and go downstairs."

Larry had been to the double-lockdown psychiatric unit many times over the past few years. Yet the moment he and Gracie were buzzed into the main area where the doors locked behind them, he knew that today would be very different. He was used to the heaviness of the room. There was a sadness, and oftentimes a hopelessness, that felt almost palpable. But as he stepped through the doors today, there was a tension and sense of danger that stopped him in his tracks.

A large man stood a few feet away—police officers on each side of him. The room was eerily silent. From the way the officers were standing with their hands open and hovering at their sides to the way the man's fists shook and the veins in his neck bulged, Larry suspected the man had likely been brought here against his will and was considered a threat to others as well as to himself. Larry instinctively took two steps back. Gracie took two steps forward. *Oh Father, please show me what to do*, he pleaded. He tried to gently pull Gracie back, but she took another step toward the man. Everything in Larry wanted to retreat, but his dog wanted to pursue.

Larry eyed the orderlies and officers. He raised his eyebrows questioningly and they responded with a slight nod. Larry took a deep breath and moved ahead a few steps, then stopped. He wanted to put himself between the man and Gracie if necessary. Gracie looked at Larry and then walked to the man's side. She stood facing him, her head just below his right fist. A horrifying image of the man hitting Gracie flashed through Larry's mind, and he adjusted his stance to intervene. But something restrained him. *Wait.*

The man opened his hand and rested his trembling fingers on Gracie's head. He stretched his fingers out, then pulled them back, awkwardly rubbing Gracie's head. Over and over his fingers stretched, then curled. Stretched, then curled. Then, to Larry's amazement, the man slowly lowered to one knee and petted her back, her chest, her shoulders. Gracie sat beside him, and he leaned his head against hers, his body relaxing and his countenance softening.

The intake staff quickly stepped in and processed the patient without needing either medication or restraints. All he needed was the steady presence of a gentle, intuitive dog. Gracie had no way of knowing how God had worked through her to diffuse a potentially dangerous situation. But Larry knew, and he would never forget it. Nor would he forget the way he had felt God's presence so strongly in that moment.

And yet less than ten minutes later, Larry and Gracie experienced a very different moment in a patient's room.

"Get that mangy dog out of here!" an elderly man with white stringy hair screamed as Larry approached. The man's leathered face twisted in disgust. "Shoo, get! Get her out of here. Get OUT!"

Larry led Gracie quickly from the room. He had learned that sometimes it's best to leave a situation before it escalates.

When Larry and Gracie got home, the phone rang. It was a woman named Lisa who wanted to become a Canines for Christ volunteer.

"I got your name and number from a nursing home I've started visiting with my Golden Retriever, Skipper," she explained. "We got Skipper after my mom died. During her illness I saw firsthand how much comfort and companionship dogs can bring people, and to honor her life I started taking Skipper to visit people in nursing homes. One of the nurses told me about your ministry, and it seems like a perfect fit. Skipper already has his Canine Good Citizen certification, so we're ready to join your team, if you'll have us."

Larry felt an instant connection to her story and set up a joint visit for the following week at the nursing home where Lisa had been volunteering. After putting the information into his calendar, he fed Gracie, then sat back down to reply to emails. One was from a heartbroken mother from California who was desperate to get help for her son.

Dear Chaplain Larry,

I am a single mom of four. We are domestic violence victims.

My youngest son suffered major abuse, and although I have tried all kinds of services and therapies, he is becoming more withdrawn and depressed and lacks the ability to care about himself, school, or other activities. His confidence is low, and he struggles to make friends. It has been mentioned that a therapy dog would benefit him greatly. He has wanted a dog for a while. My income is very small, but we homeschool, so we have time to train a dog. I am seeking help for my little boy before I lose him. He has no father in his life, and the mentor that I did find for him hurt him too. He is only 11, and as a mom I am just trying to bring my little boy back. I have looked into therapy animals before, but the wait and cost is too much. My son has asked our pastor to speak to you regarding getting him a dog. He needs help now. He needs a friend who he can trust. He loves animals. We are in protective custody, and we are afraid. Please, can you help us?

Larry closed his eyes. "Oh God, I can't imagine what this woman or her children have been through. Please shine your light into their lives and give them hope and strength. And please show me how you would have us help her."

Gracie wandered back into Larry's office. *How can we help? It sounds like the boy needs a certified service dog, but we are a therapy dog ministry.* Larry knew that most people use the terms interchangeably, but there is a difference. A service dog is trained to provide a specific service to a person, so the dog is allowed to go most everywhere with them. Since therapy dogs provide comfort and companionship, they are not afforded the same privileges as service dogs. Still, Larry believed that a well-trained therapy dog should be allowed to go wherever comfort was needed.

"This little boy needs a *service* dog," Larry said aloud, startling Gracie, who had just lain down by his feet. "He needs a companion to help him feel safe—anywhere he goes."

Larry tapped his pen on the desk. *Who do I know that has experience with service dogs?* A name formed on his lips before it had even registered in his mind. "Becky." Becky, a lovely woman with a strong faith, had been with Canines for Christ for a few years now—*and* she was certified to train service dogs. He found her contact information, called, and left a message on her phone. An hour later she returned his call, and he explained the situation.

"Let me see what I can do," Becky said. "I will reach out to my contacts and see if we can get a dog for this boy."

🐾

The next week Larry and Gracie met Lisa and Skipper outside of Arbor Oaks nursing home. Larry smiled at the handsome Golden Retriever as he bounded toward Gracie. His open-mouthed canine smile reminded Larry of Cody, the dog that had started it all.

"Thank you so much for coming today," Lisa said, shaking his hand. "And thank you, too, Gracie. Skipper and I are so happy to meet both of you." She rubbed Gracie's side, then put a hand on each dog. Lisa's outgoing, bubbly personality made Larry feel like they had been friends for years. They shared their experiences with dogs and the many ways they had seen God work through their dogs.

"Once I realized that God had given me a gift of service and that serving and helping others gives me joy, I looked for ways to use it."

"Well, I am so glad you called, Lisa. I can already tell that you and Skipper are a perfect fit for Canines for Christ."

Lisa's face brightened even more. "Me too! And I can't wait to introduce you to Bill. Skipper and I have been visiting him every week. He has had dogs his whole life but had to give up his most recent dog when he moved in here. He gets so excited to see Skipper that I've started bringing half of Skipper's breakfast with me on days when we come so that Bill can hand-feed him." Lisa pulled a plastic baggie of kibble from her purse. "Bill loves feeding Skipper and Skipper loves to eat! So everybody's happy."

Oh yes, Lisa will make a wonderful addition to the ministry.

When Larry and Lisa led their dogs through the common area of the nursing home, they were welcomed with a chorus of *oohs* and *aahs* from excited residents. Gracie and Skipper went around the room in opposite directions, Larry and Lisa following behind. Some of the residents were unresponsive, and several were noncoherent. And yet Lisa spoke to each one with kindness and respect while Skipper stood beside them, receiving touches or gently placing his paw on their lap.

"That's what I love best about him," Lisa said as she and Larry walked to a smaller room. "Skipper isn't concerned with the health or stability of someone's brain. He always just goes straight for the heart."

"Skipper's here!" an elderly gentleman in a wheelchair announced.

"Hi, Bill!" Lisa sang out, holding on to Skipper's leash as the dog made a beeline for his friend—and for the rest of his breakfast.

Lisa introduced Larry and Gracie as she pulled the baggie from her purse. Skipper sat in rapt attention in front of Bill. The moment Gracie saw Bill's hand in the baggie, she followed Skipper's lead.

"Can she have some too?" Bill asked.

Larry normally didn't allow Gracie to have food during visits, but he decided to make an exception. "Just don't get used to it, girl," he said quietly.

Bill placed several pieces of kibble on his palm and offered it to Skipper, then he reached back into the bag and gave a few pieces to Gracie. "Okay, handshake time," he said, holding his hand out. Skipper quickly placed his paw up, then down, immediately resuming his straight-as-a-board sit. When Bill presented his hand to Gracie, she gently placed her paw on it and kept it there.

Bill laughed. "Well, if you want more food, I need my hand back." Gracie got the message and sat back as straight as Skipper. For the next five minutes, Bill fed and shook paws with each dog numerous times.

When it was time to say goodbye, Larry handed Lisa a new volunteer kit, which included a T-shirt for her, a vest for Skipper, training materials, visit suggestions, and several helpful books and pamphlets. She put the vest on Skipper and then took a picture of him and Gracie. She already had two more places lined up for her and Skipper—a children's hospital and a residential facility for people fighting cancer. When Larry told her about Trinity, Lisa asked if she and Skipper could attend Dog Church the following week.

"Everyone is welcome at Dog Church," Larry assured her.

"Larry? It's Becky. I found a dog."

Larry had just sat down to dinner, but immediately got to his feet. It had been two weeks since he'd read the heartbroken mother's email and had contacted Becky about a service dog for her son. He had been praying daily about the situation, but he hadn't been expecting to hear anything this soon. He grabbed a pen and started scribbling notes on a piece of paper.

"One of my contacts found an eighteen-month-old female Aussiedoodle in Ohio. A fellow trainer was in the process of training this dog for an agency, but the placement fell through, and the dog became available. She sounds perfect. Her name is Zoey. She's on the small-to-medium side, but large enough to play and handle a busy household. Calm temperament. Intelligent. Eager to learn."

Yes, Lord, she sounds perfect.

"Becky, if you can make the arrangements to get the dog here, Canines for Christ will cover the travel costs. We will also cover your training costs—that is, if you're willing to train her." He hadn't meant to assume she would be willing to take on this project. She likely had a long list of clients. His mind began racing with alternatives to get the Aussiedoodle service dog trained.

"I'll do it—absolutely," Becky said. "I'll get her trained and certified as a service dog, and I'll apply for all the necessary documentation. But it will take several weeks."

Larry had a feeling the boy's mother would be so grateful to know a dog was coming that she wouldn't mind waiting a little longer.

"Thank you so much, Becky," Larry said, his voice thick with emotion. "I'll email the mother to let her know. Oh, and Becky? If you'd be willing, we would love to send you to California to present the dog to the family. They are in protective custody, so I'm sure there will be a lot to figure out there, but I just wanted to mention that to give you something else to think about."

"I would be honored to do that. I honestly can't imagine anything better than introducing a hurting little boy to his new best friend."

The following week, Lisa and Skipper joined Larry and Gracie, Laura and Carl with Chloe and Leah, and two other volunteer teams for Dog Church. The students were ecstatic to have six dogs in their midst. The first ten minutes were spent hugging and holding dogs, receiving canine kisses, and inviting Paws Up interactions. Larry watched with fatherly pride as Laura interacted with Willie. She had grown much more comfortable sharing her story—and her pain—with others. Larry knew it hadn't been easy for her. He and Susan had spent many hours praying with her and for her. Since meeting her that day at Walgreens, Laura had undergone several more surgeries, had been prescribed—and then discovered to have been overprescribed—many different medications, and was in constant pain and discomfort. And yet she still showed up to serve and extend God's love to others—which often helped her receive and accept God's love herself.

"This is Leah," Laura said, introducing their new dog to Willie. "We adopted her last month."

"She looks like Gracie," Willie observed.

"She's actually Gracie's sister," Laura explained. "The same mama dog gave birth to them, but Leah lived somewhere else for the past four years."

"Why did she have to live somewhere else?"

Larry noticed Laura's expression change, likely aware of Willie's ongoing prayer request to find his family. "Another family wanted her to live with them," she answered slowly, measuring her words, "but then they couldn't take care of her anymore, so they gave her back to the lady who had her when she was a puppy. The lady called us to tell us she needed a home, and we adopted her."

Willie's eyes were on Leah the entire time Laura spoke. Chloe wandered over, and he patted her head, then he clutched his hands together, and rested his elbows on his wheelchair tray. Larry subtly patted Laura's shoulder in encouragement as he walked by.

"Will Gracie sing again?" Emmeline asked loudly.

Larry quietly explained to Lisa that Gracie surprised everyone when she participated the first time they sang "Amazing Grace."

"And she continues to join in," he added.

"Well, I happen to sing a little myself," Lisa informed him. "How about I lead us in some songs and end with 'Amazing Grace'?"

"I'd say I think we just hired a praise team!"

Lisa stood in front of the group and began to sing an upbeat rendition of "Jesus Loves Me," followed by "He's Got the Whole World in His Hands." The energy in the room was higher than it had ever been. People sang and clapped along, they swayed to the beat, and a few even raised their hands in worship. Larry's heart pounded with gratitude and joy. And when Gracie began howling during the final song, the joy in Larry's heart overflowed in worship.

After sharing a message from Psalm 18 about how God always keeps his promises, Larry asked the group for prayer requests. Most everyone shared something—including Willie's continual appeal for God to help him find his family. After closing, Larry and the other volunteers had the dogs do one last round of visits. Larry and Gracie found themselves next to Laura and Leah. The two canine sisters walked side by side. When Laura got to Willie, she reached into her pocket, pulled out a small object, and handed it to him. Willie held it up, and Larry saw it was a palm-sized wooden cross.

"I have been telling my mother about you, and she asked me to give this to you," he heard Laura say.

"This is from your *mother*?" Willie spoke the last word with a reverence that made Larry tear up. "For me?"

"It is for you, to keep. And when you look at it, I want you to remember us, okay? You remember that you have people who love you."

"I will," Willie said, clutching the cross to his heart.

When he got home that day, Larry opened an email from the mother in California.

> Thank you, Brother Larry, for allowing God to use you as a sharp tool in his hand. I have been in touch with your volunteer, and she told me the wonderful news of a dog for my son! It has given him hope and something to look forward to. Although things are rough for him now, I know God is in the picture. When my son is in therapy for his trauma, he often mentions the hope of a safe and loving friend that he will soon have. Thank you for caring for a family you have never met and for giving so unselfishly to my son during this very hard time for us. It is a mother's worst nightmare that I am trying to navigate through. I am trying to hold on to every bit of light God brings into our lives to show me I am not forsaken or forgotten. His promises bring comfort to my pain. Your kindness has brought a smile to a hurting family's face. Thank you for being there for us!

Larry printed the email and left it on the top of his desk as a reminder to pray for this precious family and for the little dog named Zoey who would be joining them very soon.

🐾

A few weeks later, Larry and Gracie arrived at the Lutz Rehabilitation Center and parked in an empty spot near the front. With his ankle acting up again, he was grateful for the proximity to the entrance. He scanned the parking lot as he let Gracie out of the car. Maybe the man he was scheduled to meet hadn't arrived yet . . .

"Larry! Over here! Bruce and I got here a little early."

Larry had met Steve Kesler at church the previous Sunday when Larry and Gracie were serving as greeters in the lobby. Steve walked over and introduced himself, and Larry soon discovered that Steve could talk—a lot and very fast.

"My wife, Liz, and I are new to the area. We recently moved from Kansas, and before that we lived in Colorado. So this is our third state in three years. We loved Kansas—actually that's where I found the Lord again after forty-five years of not even thinking about him. I guess I should really say that the Lord found me, you know?"

Larry barely had a chance to decide if he was supposed to nod or shake his head. Steve continued, telling about his successful business career that ended when a bad investment cost him everything. He slipped into a dark depression until he walked into the Kansas church and felt God say, *Where have you been? It's time to get started.* In the midst of all that, he and his wife, Liz, rescued a dog named Bruce, who had been horribly mistreated and abused.

"I thought maybe we should give the dog back to the rescue, but not my Lizzy. She was determined to help Bruce feel loved and give him a home. So we worked with him, were patient with him, observed him, and determined what he needed—part of which included long runs to release pent-up energy. Bruce is part German Shepherd, part Greyhound, so he has a *lot* of energy. And he's smart as a whip. He knows more than thirty tricks and can do most of them in rapid-fire succession. Anyway, while our lives were falling apart, we were helping Bruce put his back together.

"Enough about me," Steve said. "I want to know about your ministry. I've been trying to get a job, but every door has closed so far. So I've asked God to show me what to do—how to spend my days—and then I walk in here and meet you and Gracie."

Larry could see the interest, passion, and determination in Steve's eyes. He had never met a more eager prospective volunteer. Steve offered to meet Larry anywhere anytime, and the sooner the better. So Larry suggested that Steve meet him and Gracie at the rehabilitation facility for their regular visitation time. "I'll be there!" Steve said

And true to his word, Steve was waiting there for Larry, as eager to volunteer as he had expressed in the church lobby.

"This is my boy, Bruce."

Larry patted the tall, lanky dog. He could see characteristics of both breeds in him. If ever a dog had looked intelligent, this one surely did. His ready expression and cocked head reminded Larry of an inquisitive professor trying to decipher a riddle. But when Gracie walked up to him, Bruce transformed into a lovesick puppy. Bruce began sniffing her ears, licking her face, and standing close beside her.

"I think it's love at first sight," Steve joked.

Larry quickly talked Steve through the visiting process and then led Gracie, Steve, and Bruce through the doors. It didn't take long for Steve and Bruce to catch on. Bruce's height was a blessing to many who found it easier to reach him from their wheelchairs and hospital beds. And his repertoire of tricks was a huge hit in the common room. Steve expressed genuine care and concern with each person.

"I'm hooked," Steve said as they left the facility. "This is what I'm meant to do. I know it as plainly as I know I'm talking to you. The simplicity, beauty, and power of this ministry is incredible, Larry. I want in. All in."

Steve not only started making daily visits to various sites, but he also became a certified chaplain and an approved AKC Canine Good Citizen evaluator. Within a short time, he and Bruce were spending five to six hours a day visiting people. Steve had an endless supply of energy. Not surprisingly, at year's end Steve had logged more visits than any other volunteer. And he had also become one of Larry's best friends. Steve sought out Larry's advice, insights, and prayers on a regular basis. And because Steve was so hungry to learn and grow in his faith, Larry found that his own faith was strengthened by mentoring his friend. Gracie enjoyed Bruce's company, too, and so the four of them often made visits together.

"Is there anything Steve can't do?" Susan had joked one night after dinner with Steve and Liz. "He went to twelve different facilities in one day! How is that even possible? And did I hear him right that he has some ideas on how to grow and expand the ministry?"

Larry nodded. He loved his friend, but he was often exhausted after spending a long amount of time with him. Steve far outpaced his endurance and drive. And that was just fine with Larry.

"Oh," Larry said, "Becky called me earlier today to say that Zoey is officially a service dog for the young boy in California."

"That's wonderful!" Susan exclaimed.

"Becky said Zoey took to him immediately, like she knew that he was her boy and the reason she was there. Becky spent two hours with them, making sure they knew all the commands and answering all the questions they had. She even gave them her number in case they ran into any issues. But from the smiles and tears of joy on their faces, she doesn't anticipate any issues."

"Well done, Larry Randolph," Susan said, kissing his forehead. Larry patted Gracie's head. She seemed as exhausted from keeping up with Bruce as he was from Steve. "It's been a busy day, girl. Should we head to bed?"

Gracie was on her bed before Larry even made it to the room.

CHAPTER TWENTY

TWO YEARS LATER

"Chaplain Larry, I'm the best man," Willie announced with pride. "Laura put this flower on my shirt, and Carl put this tie on me. We're getting married."

Larry smiled at the man who had finally found his family after being *unofficially* adopted by Laura and Carl two years earlier. Laura's mother, who had heard her talk about Willie's weekly prayer request for a family, suggested they "adopt" him and give him a family. The following week Laura ran the idea past Willie. "I know we're not the family you were born into, but we sure do love you and we would like to become your family. What do you think?"

Willie smiled so wide that his eyes squeezed shut. "I LIKE it!" he shouted. The following month, Willie visited Laura and Carl's home to celebrate Laura's birthday and meet his new family—including his new "granny." Willie might not share DNA, skin color, or genealogy with the Stewart family, but he had become part of their family in all the ways that mattered. And now he was serving as the best man at Laura and Carl's twenty-fifth anniversary marriage renewal ceremony, which was being held at Trinity.

The students and staff had transformed the large multipurpose room into a wedding venue with a beautiful backdrop of white curtains and pink and silver streamers. Laura and Carl's children—including Willie—were serving as bridesmaids and groomsmen. And while everyone greatly missed Chloe, who had died several months earlier, Leah and their newest dog, Louie, were both there, as well as most of the students and staff at Trinity. Several Canines for Christ teams came for the big event too.

"There's a lot of people here," Willie observed, tugging on his tie.

"And every one of them loves you, and they are so happy that Carl has such a special best man," Larry replied. "I think it's time for us to take our places. Are you ready?"

"Ready!"

Larry officiated the short ceremony—his first with such a high dog-to-human ratio. The dogs looked like ushers as they sat around the room in their red vests, with their handlers beside them. The students were quiet and focused on the ceremony—until Larry said, "You may kiss the bride," at which point the room erupted in applause, shouts, laughter, and barks. Afterward, the humans enjoyed cake and punch, and the dogs enjoyed lots of belly rubs and attention. It was a full and wonderful day, highlighting the truth that God had turned Canines for Christ into a beautiful and ever-expanding family.

🐾

A week after officiating Laura and Carl's vow renewal, Larry was in his office returning emails when Susan called out to him. "Larry! Come see what's happened."

Larry and Gracie hurried to the family room, where Susan was holding the TV remote. *She's safe*, he reassured himself, surprised by how quickly his mind flashed back to five years earlier. But when Larry looked at the news banner on the TV, his relief vanished.

A mass shooting at Pulse Nightclub in Orlando. Multiple fatalities reported.

"Oh Lord, help them," Larry prayed aloud.

Gracie sat on the sofa between Larry and Susan as they watched coverage of the tragedy. She laid her head on Larry's lap and sighed.

"I know, girl, we'll go."

Twenty minutes later, he was making arrangements with Steve for the two of them and their dogs to travel to Orlando to offer whatever comfort and support they could. The news was initially reporting more than forty fatalities, with at least fifty more wounded. (Later, the final toll would turn out to be forty-nine killed and sixty-eight injured.) Larry and Steve spent the next day praying for the heartbroken families and friends, for the wounded, and for the community left reeling in the wake of such evil. After speaking with a Canines for Christ volunteer who lived in the area and contacting several other crisis response teams, Larry and Steve planned to travel to Orlando early the following week.

🐾

Five days later, Larry and Steve led Gracie and Bruce into the hospital where the majority of the victims and survivors had been taken. While they both felt a slight hesitation about how they would be received, they were resolved and resolute to their task. They were there not to preach or persuade, but simply to bring God's presence. They were there to love the people who were affected by the tragedy. Gracie and Bruce ministered to grieving families in the lobby, anxious loved ones in waiting rooms, traumatized patients in the ICU, and heartbroken citizens in the chapel and at the memorial that had been set up across the street for the forty-nine whose lives had been taken.

Larry was honored to pray with several people and to simply be present as many more buried their faces in Gracie's fur and sobbed. He didn't have any answers, but he was grateful to get to provide a safe place for people to process their pain and grieve such a devastating loss. It was a long day, but neither Gracie nor Bruce showed signs of slowing down. They were resolved to stay with everyone who needed them.

And while Bruce was normally a bit of a ham, today he was quiet and reserved—which was true of Gracie too. It was clear the dogs knew something very bad had happened, and they acted accordingly. They sat for hugs, lay down to snuggle, and stayed steady as the tides of grief ebbed and flowed.

Larry and Steve drove out of Orlando as the sun sank below the horizon, and it was a quiet ride home. Both dogs slept, and both men were lost in their thoughts. But inside his heart, Larry kept thanking God for allowing him to play a small role in bringing comfort and solace to hurting people.

🐾

Over the next few weeks, a heaviness settled over Larry. He thought often of the people he'd met in Orlando. He prayed for them and stayed in contact with the Canines for Christ volunteers in the area. One warm summer morning, he walked into his office with Gracie to spend time in prayer and tried to center his heart and mind on God. He began by writing a prayer in his journal.

Lord, I am so weary. My physical and emotional strength is weak today. Please refresh me with new strength so that I can be present with others and give your words of encouragement, hope, love, and kindness to everyone I meet. The needs are so great, and my strength is so small. But your strength is limitless. Please fill me with your presence and strength today.

He read several passages in Psalms and spent some more time in prayer before turning on his computer and clicking the email icon.

The first email he opened was from a Canines for Christ volunteer in New Jersey. His mouth slacked open as he read about a therapy dog named Ezekiel—whose name means "God strengthens."

Hi, Chaplain Larry, my name is Mary. I wanted to send you a note of thanks for starting this ministry and to tell you about our therapy dog, Ezekiel.

Ezekiel, our white Boxer, was only three weeks old when we found out he was deaf. We had to make the decision of whether or not to go ahead and adopt him. It was extremely hard, but not because he was deaf. It was hard because my husband, Tom, was battling cancer, and we didn't know how it was going to work out. But we both felt like we were supposed to bring Ezekiel home.

He instantly gravitated to my husband, who had IVs administered twice a day by nurses. Ezekiel stayed in my husband's lap most of the day. We knew that there was something very different about this goofy, deaf white Boxer. We named him Ezekiel because it means "God strengthens." We knew he had a special mission on this earth. He had compassion and an empathy that we had never seen in a dog before.

We started teaching Ezekiel American Sign Language when he was eight weeks old. He caught on extremely quickly. At 6 months old we enrolled him in obedience school, and then we started exposing him to all kinds of situations, people, and other dogs. Two years later, we made an appointment for Ezekiel to take the Canine Good Citizen test. I gave him all the commands in ASL, and he passed with flying colors.

We then reached out to Canines for Christ, after learning about the ministry from a friend, and we joined. We started going to nursing homes, convalescent centers, independent living centers, and many other places. Ezekiel also comes to school with me every Friday and ministers to the special-needs kids I work with. Ezekiel has been to deaf schools where the kids are able to sign to him, and they get so excited when he understands. And he even serves with me at church. We know Ezekiel was sent by God to minister to people. Our next venture will be visiting a juvenile prison.

Our Ezekiel has impacted so many lives, even if that means making someone smile for a minute or distracting them from their pain for a moment. To me, that is what this ministry is all about. Comforting those in need and just being present. I don't know where my husband would be today if it weren't for Ezekiel. I know God sent him to us. I am so grateful Tom is in remission now and has been cancer-free for three years. Thank you for obeying God and starting this wonderful ministry.

Mary and Tom

"Thank you, Lord," Larry prayed, surprised and grateful at the speed at which God had answered his prayer for strength. "Thank you for allowing me to be a part of this. And thank you for strengthening me through this letter. Bless Mary and Tom and Ezekiel, and let many encounter your love through them."

Larry had walked into his office feeling burdened by the needs of the world—needs he felt incapable of meeting. And through Mary and Tom's email and several others like it, God was reminding him to look up. To remember that God is the one who meets the needs of his children. That God is the one who raises up people to be his hands and feet. Larry's heart felt strengthened in ways he couldn't have imagined just an hour earlier.

After feeding Gracie, Larry was feeling so energized and his ankle pain was so low that he decided to take her for a walk. They had walked almost a mile when Gracie stopped to watch a large sandhill crane standing on someone's driveway. Larry chuckled at the memory of one-year-old Gracie chasing a crane while dragging a wrought-iron chair behind her.

"You've come a long way, girl," he said, praising her for passing the bird without giving chase. "Over the years we've learned a lot about what to chase after and what to let go, haven't we?"

🐾

Six months later, Gracie and Bruce were interacting with the students and staff of LYF (Learning Your Function) Inc.—an adult day program for people with intellectual and developmental disabilities.

"Hi, Chaplain Larry!" a jovial young man called out. "Hi, Gracie dog!"

"Bruce is here!"

"Chaplain Steve is here!"

A group playing T-ball heard the greetings and abandoned their game for Gracie and Bruce. The two dogs walked among the group of thirty students gathered outside for their large group time. When Bruce started entertaining people with his repertoire of tricks, Gracie walked over to a quiet young woman sitting by herself, making lines in the sandy soil with her finger. She looked up at Gracie and then at Larry.

"I . . . I don't want to . . . to play," she said, casting a nervous look at Larry.

Gracie sniffed the ground where the woman was digging, then sat beside her.

"Oh, that's okay," Larry assured her. "Gracie just wanted to come say hi to you."

The woman looked at Gracie. Her expression was confused delight. "She . . . she waa . . . wants to say hi to . . . me?"

Larry's heart went out to the shy woman.

"She sure does, and so do I. What's your name?"

"Mi . . . Michelle," she said, her eyes focused on the dirt.

"Hi, Michelle, I'm Larry and this is my dog, Gracie. Thank you for letting us visit with you. Gracie sometimes likes to have a quiet break when things get loud, and I know she's glad she has a friend to spend some quiet time with."

"I . . . I like quiet too. I . . . don't like T . . . T-ball."

Larry leaned against the tree while Michelle held a stick up to show Gracie. She nosed it but didn't take it from Michelle, who began dragging the stick back and forth through the dirt. Gracie watched for several minutes then began pawing at the dirt. Michelle's head shot up.

"She's digging like . . . like me!"

"You're friends, and she likes doing things with you."

Michelle squeezed her eyes shut and hugged Gracie. "I love you, Gracie. You . . . you are my friend."

Eventually, Larry and Steve spent an hour inside the facility, going in and out of classrooms. While some of the students were fearful of dogs and didn't want them to come close, most of them rushed toward the dogs when they entered the room. Bruce and Gracie were a good team. Bruce thrived on entertaining, distracting, and bringing laughter while Gracie seemed more inclined to draw near, sit close, and bring comfort.

"They really are the perfect therapy dog duo," Larry commented to Steve on their way out of the LYF building.

Steve was heading out to make at least four more visits that day, but Larry decided to take Gracie home. He detected a slight limp as they walked to the car, enough for him to know that she needed to rest. And at almost ten years of age, he didn't want to push her.

"You did good work today, girl. Let's go home."

Gracie's ears raised at the word *home*. She jumped into the car and curled into a ball on the back seat. Larry knew she loved her work but because she was getting older, he needed to think about cutting back some. *Maybe we both just need a good night's rest.*

🐾

"Sister Agnes, you look beautiful," Larry said later that summer. He and Susan each gave her a gentle hug, then led Gracie into her small home.

She waved off the compliment. "I look like a tired old woman, but I sure am glad to see you three."

They all took a seat in their usual places—Larry on the small sofa, Susan at the kitchen table, and Agnes on her recliner, with Gracie's head on her lap. Gracie had rallied the day after their visit to LYF but continued to show signs of slowing down. Thankfully, today's visit with Agnes didn't require much from Gracie except sitting at the kind woman's feet.

It had been three months, and they had a lot of catching up to do, including her most recent hospital stay, as well as the latest news out of Tall Pines. But after patiently answering Larry's and Susan's questions, Agnes placed a pillow behind her back, rubbed her favorite spot on top of Gracie's head, looked at Larry, and said, "Now, tell me what's been going on with your ministry. Take me outside of my walls and tell me what God's doing through you."

Larry loved the way she put that and was happy to oblige.

"Well, can you believe we've started adding international

volunteers? We now have volunteers in Canada, Lithuania, Germany, South Africa, the Netherlands, and the UK."

Agnes's eyes grew round with surprised delight.

"How in the world did that happen? How did they find you?"

"They all found us online—through the computer," he clarified. "We have a website now and social media pages."

"Joan has a computer and showed me the Facebook site. I don't know how to use it, but she likes it because she can see her grandkids' pictures. Do you put pictures of your dogs on Facebook?"

"We do," Larry answered. "A volunteer helps us with all of that and we are just so thankful that people are finding us. So now we have volunteers in thirty-five states and six countries. They all affirm our statement of faith, many of them have become certified chaplains, each one receives our training materials and resources, and all our volunteers desire to bring God's love to the world through therapy dogs."

"That is just wonderful." Sister Agnes beamed. Gracie's head still rested on her bony lap, her eyes closed and her body so relaxed that Larry suspected she had fallen asleep. "God is expanding his reach through you. Well done, Larry and Susan and Gracie." One eye opened, looked up at the nun, then quickly closed again.

"And thank *you*, Agnes," Larry said, his words thick with emotion. "You were the first person we visited, and I believe God brought us to you for a reason. You have always been such a source of encouragement and prayer for us, and we are so grateful to you. You will always be a special part of this ministry."

Agnes's eyes began to tear up. Larry had expected her to wave his words away, but she simply said, "Thank you for that."

As they were leaving her house, Larry glanced at the TV that had been on but set to mute during their visit.

"Looks like that hurricane is going to hit south of here," Agnes said, turning up the volume. "But I imagine they will still want to evacuate us—hurricanes are the worst part about living in Florida."

They spent several minutes watching the latest weather forecast as Hurricane Irma churned in the Gulf of Mexico. After getting Agnes's word that she would heed any evacuation orders and assuring her she was welcome at their house if she needed somewhere to go, Larry and Susan returned home, where they began making their own hurricane preparations.

🐾

A week later, Larry and Steve took Gracie and Bruce to minister to people in a hurricane evacuation shelter. Tampa had been spared a direct hit, but the Florida Keys, along with southwest and central Florida, had been hit hard, and many people had been displaced by the storm. In the shelter, Gracie and Bruce brought smiles and squeals of laughter from the children, and provided a respite and moment of reprieve for the adults to process and express some of their fears and feelings. Being able to offer people a listening ear and a loving dog to pet might seem like small things to some, but Larry had seen firsthand numerous times just how big these small things can feel to people.

But he had no way of knowing just how important those gifts would be just five months later when an unthinkable tragedy occurred four hours south of them in Parkland, Florida.

He and Susan watched in horror as video of high school students fleeing from Marjory Stoneman Douglas High School filled the TV screen. "Multiple fatalities, many wounded. Nineteen-year-old suspected gunman taken into custody."

"Show us what you would have us do," Larry prayed. "Let us

bring your love into the midst of this horrible situation. Shine your light, Lord, and bring good, even in the midst of such an evil act."

Three days later, Larry, Steve, Gracie, and Bruce headed to Parkland. A Canines for Christ crisis response team, consisting of three additional teams from the Tampa area and one from Fort Lauderdale, would join them at the Parkland Recreational Center.

When they pulled in just after noontime, they got out and walked the dogs to a nearby memorial area where a sea of flowers, balloons, cards, drawings, stuffed animals, and photos were displayed.

Seventeen photos of beautiful children.

Seventeen lives taken.

Seventeen families devastated.

Larry knelt before Gracie and began to pray for the Canines for Christ group.

"Father, we are here as your servants to bring love, kindness, comfort, hope, and peace to everyone we encounter. Love through us. Reach through us. Minister through us. Help us provide a ministry of presence—your presence and your spirit. Evil cannot stand against you. Please bring your light and goodness to this place."

The teams dispersed to make themselves available to anyone and everyone who came to the memorial. Many people stopped to pet Gracie. Some parents told Larry of their connection to someone who had died, but most were quiet. Larry didn't say much other than to pray with people or tell them how sorry he was for the pain they were experiencing. Gracie did most of the work, providing her quiet, steady presence as the grieving tried to make sense of such a senseless act.

A young girl named Alice sat on the sidewalk in front of Gracie.

She was holding a picture she had drawn of seventeen angels in the sky, looking over a field of flowers and balloons.

"My babysitter got shot," she told Gracie. "She's okay, but her friends died."

Alice's mother smiled sadly at Larry. "She loves dogs," she said softly.

Gracie lay down beside Alice. The young girl put her hand on Gracie's chest and watched it rise and fall with each breath. Alice didn't speak or move. She just watched her hand go up and down. After several minutes, she got up, patted Gracie on the head, and went to add her drawing to the outpouring of love in the memorial area.

When the sun set, the Canines for Christ teams headed to a hotel to get some sleep. They were up the next morning well before sunrise to drive to Calvary Church in Fort Lauderdale for the victims' memorial service. Almost everyone Larry met accepted his offer of prayer, and several asked for information about joining Canines for Christ. They wanted to honor their loved one by offering comfort and help to others.

🐾

It took Gracie several days of rest after the Parkland trip before she was able to resume regular visits to Trinity and LYF Inc., and the occasional hospital and nursing home. Given the ankle pain he had been experiencing lately, Larry appreciated the slower pace as well. Thankfully, Steve and Bruce showed no signs of slowing down; if anything, they were ramping up their visits. So much so that Bruce received the AKC Therapy Dog Supreme title, which was given to dogs who had made more than six hundred visits. Actually, Bruce had far exceeded that number, but that was the highest title they had to offer. Steve was honored by the recognition, then quickly went back to work with Bruce.

"I think it's time to call Denise about another puppy," Larry said to Susan a week after they returned from Parkland. "I can't imagine another dog as suited for this work as Gracie, but I also know she won't be able to do this forever. And I want her to be able to train a new dog to take over for her."

Even as Larry said the words, he found it hard to think of doing this without his Gracie. She was his girl. His partner. But she was getting older—they both were, and he needed to keep his eyes on the future of the ministry. It was time to get a game plan together for the next decade. One that would involve training Gracie's replacement, as well as lining up people to take over for him and Susan. Knowing that the ministry was never his to hold but to shepherd made the idea of handing it over to someone else someday much easier to think about.

Yet, while he was excited at the prospect of a new puppy in the house, he just couldn't imagine loving another dog as much as he loved Gracie.

🐾

Denise had been ecstatic to tell Larry and Susan that a litter had been born on New Year's Day and invited them to come out and meet the puppies. A week after calling Denise to arrange the visit, they stood in one of her kennels with ten adorable six-week-old white Lab puppies.

"How will we ever choose?" Susan wondered aloud, laughing as four of the puppies tumbled over each other and landed in a pile at her feet.

Larry spent time with each one—playing with them, holding

them, and making eye contact. He held a medium-sized female up to his face and stared into her eyes. She stared right back, her soulful eyes never moving from his. Her gentle nature reminded him of Gracie. He and Susan had already decided on the name Sadie.

"I think we found our Sadie," he said to Susan, as the puppy kissed his nose. "I hope that means you agree, Sadie!" He chuckled, hugging the puppy close.

Two weeks later, they brought Sadie home—and once again Denise had insisted they take the puppy as a gift. "I believe in the work God is doing through you, and I am honored to play a small part in that," she had said.

"Your big sister is going to love you," Larry told Sadie, curled up in his lap.

They had taken Gracie by the kennel to meet Sadie the previous week, and it had gone well. Both dogs seemed excited to meet the other, and Larry knew Gracie would love being a big sister.

But he was wrong that it would be love at first sight. Meeting a puppy at a kennel was one thing. Having an energetic puppy at your house *all the time* was a very different situation. Larry was surprised at Gracie's uncharacteristically aloof behavior the first few weeks they had Sadie. Most of the time she tried to ignore the fluffy puppy who was desperate to play with her. If that didn't work, Gracie would give a warning grumble.

"You are and will always be the queen of this castle, Gracie," Larry tried to reassure her. "Sadie isn't here to take your place; she's here to be your friend and take some of the burden off of you."

If only Gracie could understand. But since she couldn't, Larry kept Sadie in a small crate in their room at night to give her more time to warm up to the puppy. It took a few months, but Gracie eventually started seeking Sadie out to play, sharing her toys with her, and taking naps beside her. Within three months, the two dogs were inseparable.

"See, Gracie," Larry said, as they all lounged by the pool, "You are still the queen around here."

Suddenly, the queen began frantically barking at a frog who had breached the perimeter.

"I am forever at your service, Queen Gracie," her loyal subject said, scooping the frog into a net and releasing it in the nearby bushes.

CHAPTER TWENTY-ONE

"Gracie had a puppy!" Richard heralded, spotting Larry with Gracie and Sadie in Trinity's lobby.

He clapped his hands together and ran back into the multi-purpose room. Moments later a dozen students stood in the doorway. Larry had begun training six-month-old Sadie by taking her to the mall, home improvement stores, and church, but this was her first official Canines for Christ in-training visit. And he couldn't think of a better place to introduce her to the work she would be doing as a therapy dog than Dog Church at Trinity.

"Puppy Gracie!" Emmeline squealed.

Teachers and helpers moved the students back into the room, where they spread out in a large circle so everyone could see the new arrival. Larry introduced Sadie and explained that she would be helping Gracie make visits and eventually take over when

Gracie retired someday. He knew that most of the students didn't understand what retirement meant, but he felt it was important to begin to prepare them for the changes that would be coming.

Gracie moved around her circle of friends, greeting each one with a soulful look, an upheld paw, a gentle kiss, or her presence. Her demeanor was calm. Her steps careful.

And then there was Sadie. The puppy was energy and happiness in fur. She bounced and wiggled. Flopped and rolled. She zigged and zagged, and wanted to greet everyone at once. And yet, somehow, she still managed to look at people with the same soulful eyes as Gracie. Sadie still had a lot to learn, but she had a way about her—an instinct—Larry knew was God-given. It was nothing he could teach her to do. It was just in her. And watching his puppy interact with the Trinity students only confirmed his belief.

But what amazed him more was watching Gracie teach Sadie. After several minutes of Sadie's adorable puppy antics, Gracie walked over and nosed her as if trying to get her attention. Sadie play-bowed excitedly, but when Gracie didn't respond, she tilted her head to the side and watched Gracie walk to Ed, who was sitting on the floor. Larry smiled at the memory of Ed escorting him and Cody around Trinity that first day. The perpetually smiling man had grown to love Gracie as much as he had loved Cody. He patted his lap and Gracie walked right to him, with Sadie following close behind. Ed's lips parted in joy as he greeted the puppy with one hand, while keeping the other on Gracie's side. Larry wished he could understand the man's vocalizations, but from the look of delight on his face, Larry had a pretty good idea what he was communicating.

A few minutes later, the other volunteer teams arrived, and

Dog Church officially began. Larry stood in the back with Gracie and Sadie while Lisa led everyone in singing. The students loved singing "Every Praise" by Hezekiah Walker. Then Lisa transitioned to "Jesus Loves Me" and ended with "He's Got the Whole World in His Hands." The routine had become so familiar and such a part of Dog Church that Larry couldn't imagine the service without it. After music time was over, Larry walked to the front with Gracie and shared a short message based on Jesus' encounter with the woman at the well.

"Jesus wasn't in a rush," he told the forty students gathered in the large room. "He wasn't too busy or too important to talk to the woman. In fact, Jesus went out of his way to sit and talk with her. Just like he wants to sit and talk with you. Jesus is always with you, and he always has time for you." Larry scanned the room where six Canines for Christ dogs were lying or sitting beside the students—not rushed, not too busy, just happy to be present with their friends. *Jesus in fur.*

After finishing his reflection, Larry asked the students to share their praises from the week before—how God had answered their prayers and also to thank him for all the ways he provided for them. Hands went up all over the room as everyone wanted to share a praise.

"My doctor's visit went good," Emmeline said.

"I got to see my mom," Richard reported.

"There are no storms today," Alex, their self-appointed weatherman, shared.

Praises continued for the next ten minutes, then Larry asked for prayer requests.

"Laura is coming to see me today," Willie shared. "I ask God to keep her safe in her car when she drives."

Laura and Carl had moved to Palm Coast, Florida, so she could be closer to the Mayo Clinic doctors and specialists treating her, but she stayed in close contact with Willie and made the two-and-a-half-hour drive every few months to visit him—and always came by Larry and Susan's house too.

During one of their visits, Larry commented on the lightness and joy he observed in Laura. "I finally forgave him," Laura said, referring to the drunk driver who had caused her accident several years earlier. "After years of anger and resentment, I finally laid it all down and surrendered it to God." Her heartfelt declaration brought a wave of gratitude and emotion to Larry's heart.

And he wasn't surprised at all when several weeks later, Laura and Carl started a Palm Coast chapter of Canines for Christ and quickly went to work making visits with Leah and their younger dog, Louie.

"We will definitely pray for Laura's safe travels," Larry assured Willie.

Several more prayer requests were made for illness, friends, family members who had died years earlier, for good weather, and Emmeline asked for prayer for a toothache. After Larry led everyone in prayer, Lisa came back up front and led everyone in singing "Amazing Grace"—including Gracie who, like she did most weeks, howled along to her song.

Larry's heart was full as he left Trinity. He never could have imagined what God had planned for them when he'd walked in through the glass doors with Cody all those years ago. Sweet Cody was gone now, Gracie was soon to retire, and yet in many ways the work was just getting started. And would continue with Sadie, with the other teams, with the people who had been receiving God's love week after week and were now extending it to others.

"Will you take Sadie with you to LYF tomorrow?" Susan asked on the way home.

Larry and Steve had started a Bible study at LYF, which became so popular that they added a monthly chapel service that followed the format of Dog Church at Trinity. However, where Trinity's service consisted of thirty to forty students, the chapel service at LYF included students from all four campuses, which meant there were between two hundred and three hundred students there each month. It was a big endeavor, but it was worth every moment of planning and preparing. Seeing the joy on the faces of people as they worshipped God without judgment, without being told they were too loud or too distracting, was a highlight of Larry's month. The volunteers loved the service as much as the students.

"I think I might just take Gracie tomorrow," Larry answered, thinking it would be better to introduce Sadie to the smaller Bible study groups first. "I think we'll try chapel next month."

"Don't forget we have a video call with the Powells tonight," Susan reminded him.

Larry smiled at the mention of the couple who had been a direct answer to their prayers. A few months before they added Sadie to their family, Larry and Susan had begun praying for a younger like-minded couple who could eventually take over the ministry. While they had hundreds of wonderful volunteers in the ministry, they knew what was required to oversee such a large international ministry, and they began earnestly asking God to show them who should step into their roles. And then a woman in Texas called.

"Hi, Chaplain Larry, I'm Jill Powell. I'm here with my husband, Ross, and we just listened to a podcast and heard you talk about Canines for Christ. And we were blown away. We've been praying for weeks about finding some way to serve God with our dogs. We've been entering our dog, Haley, in agility competitions and winning ribbons and loving it, but recently we started feeling like there was more God wanted us to do. So we started praying together, and God led us to you.

"I had reached out to a few other therapy dog organizations, but nothing seemed to fit. Until we heard you talk about Canines for Christ. We are taking Haley to get the AKC Canine Good Citizen test next week and will submit an application right after so we can join the ministry. I am just so excited and thankful that God has answered our prayer. This is so much bigger than winning ribbons in agility. This is our opportunity to be ambassadors for Christ alongside our beloved Haley."

Jill's energy and passion were infectious. He put the call on speakerphone so Susan could hear, and the two couples spent thirty minutes talking and getting to know each other. Within weeks, Jill and Ross were taking Haley to an elementary school to serve as a reading buddy for at-risk youth and children who needed a little extra help learning to read. They fell in love with the program and the concept of Canines for Christ and reached out to their local church to see if others might want to join them in creating a Canines for Christ chapter in San Antonio.

The chapter grew to more than thirty teams within a year and began establishing relationships with The Salvation Army, local law enforcement agencies, foster/adoption agencies, and the YMCA. As Larry and Susan continued to get to know the Powells over the next year, they asked them to serve on the Canines for Christ board and soon began delegating more and more responsibilities to them. God was making it clear to Larry and Susan that he had chosen Jill and Ross to take over someday. For the time being, Larry felt God was still asking him to oversee the ministry, but it was a comfort to have a succession plan in place.

Gracie and Sadie stirred in the back seat, somehow knowing that they were almost home. "I look forward to hearing about the Powells' new dog, Mollie," Larry said. "Apparently, Mollie was found on the side of the road without tags, a microchip, or an owner. Jill believes she was sent to them by God and says she has the most gentle and kind disposition. She's already making plans for her to become a therapy dog."

Susan turned into their driveway and parked in the garage. Gracie and Sadie jumped out of the back seat and ran into the house. Gracie managed to keep up with Sadie, the puppy's energy rubbing off on the older dog.

"She's done you good, girl," Larry said, giving Gracie a treat and then handing one to Sadie. "Now let's go outside and make sure there are no frogs swimming in your pool."

🐾

The second morning of 2020 was just beginning to dawn as Gracie followed Larry into his office. Christmas had come and gone in a whirlwind of activity and celebration. Larry had loved every moment he spent with family, but he was also grateful for the early morning quiet time—moments spent with God and Gracie. He sat at his desk and opened his Bible and his journal. As his faithful dog curled up at his feet and closed her eyes, Larry stared through the window into the promise and possibilities of a new year, then began writing.

Father God, I don't know what this year will bring, but I do know that you are in control and you will use all things for your glory. As I reflect back on the past thirteen years with Canines for Christ, I am humbled by the growth of the ministry and the wonderful people you have brought on this journey with me. Countless lives have been touched by your amazing love. Thank you for calling me to start this ministry, and thank you for giving me the courage to obey. I look forward to whatever you have planned this year for Canines for Christ, for my life, and for the world. I surrender my life to you and give you all the praise and glory.

Larry paused and looked at his sleeping dog. Her nose twitched slightly, and she made a contented sound. His heart swelled with love and gratitude for his dog, who had made a difference in so many people's lives. He picked up his pen and continued writing.

Thank you for Gracie. She will turn twelve this year and is showing signs of her age. She is slow moving and sometimes has a hard time getting up, but overall she is good. She still loves to swim, walk, and play with Sadie. Help me as I begin to phase her out of ministry visits this year and start using Sadie more. Lord, I don't think there will ever be another dog like Gracie. She has been the perfect dog for this ministry—and for me. Her calm and gentle personality and consistent stamina to work long hours have enabled me to minister to countless people over the years. Only you, Lord, know how much time she has left, but help me to treasure every day with her and be

grateful for each day I get to spend with her. Thank you
for bringing your amazing Grace into our lives.

After reading a passage in Luke, Larry leaned back in his chair and watched the sunrise of a new year brighten the sky. Along with looking forward in anticipation of all God may have in store, he allowed his mind to wander back over how far they had come.

A montage of memories splashed across the screens in his mind, his heart reacting to each one. "You were with me through each one, Father," he prayed aloud, his fingers trailing along the sleek fur on Gracie's back. "You were holding me, leading me, always beside me—just like Gracie is with me." Gracie stood up and nosed Larry's hand. Her swaying tail and raised ears signaled that Sadie was up and it was time for breakfast. Larry closed his Bible and patted Gracie's back.

"All right, girl, today is Sadie's first visit without you, so let's make sure she's fed and then run off some of her energy."

Gracie's eyes were focused on him as if she clearly understood his every word. "You've taught her well, Gracie," he said as they walked to the office door. He paused and knelt in front of her. "My beautiful girl, you've done good. You've done very, very good." He kissed her nose. "I love you, Gracie."

Epilogue

GRACIE OFFICIALLY RETIRED IN JUNE 2021, after ministering to people for nearly thirteen years. She remained a loving and faithful companion to Larry, sitting at his feet every morning as he spent time with God, until she passed peacefully into heaven on July 5, 2023. Larry and Susan considered every day with her a gift, and they still thank God for blessing them with his amazing Grace.

Sadie stepped into her big sister's role and continues her legacy of being Jesus in fur to people, as all of the Canines for Christ dogs do.

While therapy dog visits dropped off significantly at the beginning of the pandemic, volunteers quickly found creative ways to engage in virtual visits with people. Dog Church even went virtual and expanded in the process as the new format allowed people to log in from a distance. They kept their format of praise and worship songs, a message from Chaplain Larry, praise reports, and prayer requests. And Dog Church continues to be the highlight of many people's weeks.

When visits resumed in person, the need was great. Canines for Christ dogs and their handlers stepped in to provide a supportive presence for medical personnel, students, teachers, parents, and law enforcement, as well as people in nursing homes, hospitals, prisons, rehabilitation facilities, and grief centers.

Of course, sometimes it is a Canines for Christ volunteer who finds themself in need of support. Such was the case for Steve when he had to say goodbye for now to his beloved Bruce—who made 16,478 therapy dog visits in his lifetime! And for Laura, who was heartbroken when she had to say goodbye for now to her precious Leah. Their losses were felt far and wide throughout the Canines for Christ community. And yet their community rallied around them in support and prayer. Steve now works with a beautiful Golden Retriever named Ginger, and Laura and Carl welcomed another white Lab named Ella, who is learning a lot from her big brother, Louie.

In addition to many new dogs and volunteers, Canines for Christ added a junior handler program in May of 2021, which allows children ages twelve to eighteen to serve with their dogs. The program was created by Jill Powell and Christina Jones and already has more than forty participants, each of whom receive their own junior handler cards and shirts, their own newsletter, tips for engaging others in conversation, and video instruction on how to teach their dog fun tricks.

In addition to starting the junior handler program, Jill Powell—along with her husband, Ross, and several generous volunteers—mobilized to offer support to the community of Uvalde, Texas, in May of 2022 after the shooting tragedy there. Canines for Christ volunteers arrived in a community reeling in shock, disbelief, heartache, and trauma. Their dogs stood steadfast and sure as they let people sob into their fur and provided moments of laughter for children. The dogs accompanied the bereaved to funerals, they sat outside of memorial services, and when summer ended, they accompanied terrified students back into classrooms all across the community.

Ross Powell summarized his experience in a post he shared on the ministry website:

> As the tragic events of May 24, 2022, unfolded, I knew in my spirit that Canines 4 Christ would be involved in the healing process. Having had a long-term relationship with Amanda, the local Salvation Army coordinator, Jill and I reached out to offer teams from our local San Antonio chapter to serve in any capacity she saw fit. Amanda immediately said yes and asked us to have teams on site in Uvalde on Wednesday—less than 24 hours after the tragedy claimed the lives of 21 children and adults.
>
> With Jill's supernatural ability to organize people and groups in some of the most stressful and overwhelming situations, she had seven teams deployed within 12 hours of Amanda's request. By the end of the week, 16 teams had ministered to family members of the victims, law enforcement officers from numerous agencies, and the community at large.

But little did we know that an even harder assignment awaited us . . .

On Saturday, May 28th, we received a request to send teams to a funeral home in Uvalde—where the first of many visitation services and funerals would begin on Monday. Once again, Jill jumped into action and recruited teams to be on site from noon to 9 p.m. Monday through Friday.

She and I traveled there on Tuesday, and that is when my life was forever changed for the better.

During our 90-minute drive, I prayed for strength, wisdom, and discernment to help the people of Uvalde, and the Spirit showed up in an overwhelming and indescribable fashion.

As we stood outside the funeral home greeting visitors and family members, I could feel the prompting of the Holy Spirit to reach out to people standing in different locations in the funeral home—it was like I was on a leash being led, just like Mollie.

One family I felt compelled to talk with asked me to enter the chapel where their precious child lay at rest and heartbroken people grieved. Allowing Mollie and me into the most inner sanctum of their grief and sadness had a profound effect on me, and I will never be the same.

The peace I felt from the Spirit in the midst of this encounter allowed me to show the love of Christ to

complete strangers. I have never felt the presence of
the Holy Spirit as strongly as I did that day, and I long
to have him that close on a daily basis.

Blessings, Ross

Canines for Christ teams continue to serve the community of
Uvalde and have been a source of comfort and hope for so many.

While several teams continue to serve in Texas, others have
mobilized in Southwest Florida to offer comfort and support to
those impacted by Hurricane Ian. As soon as the weather cleared,
volunteers—even some who themselves had been affected by the
storm—headed to storm-ravaged areas to visit people in shelters,
offer first responders a moment of calm in the midst of chaos, and
pray with those who desired prayer.

As Canines for Christ continued to grow, Larry found himself
asking God to provide even more teams so they could serve wherever and whenever a need arose. And yet, even he was surprised
in the spring of 2022 when a couple from Davalia Ministries
approached him at a conference about the possibility of a joint
venture with their ministry. Within months of that first meeting,
Caninos para Cristo was launched with a mission of attracting,
connecting, inspiring, and mobilizing dog lovers in Spanish-
speaking Latino communities to serve others and share God's
unconditional love. Their hope is to reach all of Latin America
and anywhere Spanish is spoken, to bring people closer to the heart
of God—one paw at a time.

And yet, God wasn't done. Just months after the launch of
Caninos para Cristo, Larry received a call from a ministry in South
Africa wanting to talk about a possible partnership.

Larry continues to trust God to lead and provide, and rests in the knowledge that if this newest partnership is God's will for them, then he will work out all the details.

Even as Larry and Susan begin to step back and hand off ministry responsibilities to the Powells and other ministry leaders, they continue to look ahead with joy and hopefulness. Every day, as Larry sits in the quiet of the morning, he prays for the ministry he loves so much—asking God to continue to open doors for them to reach more people with comfort and hope; praying for their volunteers, those they will minister to, and the dogs who bring Jesus in fur to people; and praising God for allowing him to be a part of a ministry defined by God's presence and love.

As Larry rubs Sadie's velvety-soft head, he can't help but think of Gracie and be in awe of what God can do through a willing heart and a wagging tail.

Floppy-eared Gus, the dog who
first captured Larry's heart. (1986)

Larry and puppy Gracie in 2008.
Little did they know what adventures
lay ahead.

Photo Gallery

Sister Agnes. (2008)

Gracie and Cody. (2009)

Gracie's beautiful smile. (2010)

Gracie continues to comfort Susan
after helping to save her life during
a terrifying seizure. (2011)

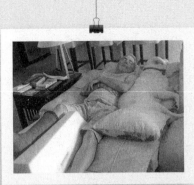

Larry and Gracie rest up after Larry's surgery. (2014)

Following his surgery, Larry is welcomed back with a party! (2014)

Dog Church in action! (2014)

Chaplain Lisa and Skipper.
(2015)

Gracie visiting a children's
cancer center. (2015)

Susan and Larry with family in 2016.
(Can you spot Gracie?)

Larry, Susan, Gracie, and puppy Sadie. (2018)

Steve and therapy dog Bruce making a new friend at church. (February 2018)

Mary and Ezekiel. (2022)

Canines for Christ serving
in Uvalde, Texas. (2022)

Laura, Willie, and Carl. (May 2022)

Laura with Louie and Ella. (2022)

Sadie and Gracie enjoying downtime in one
of their favorite places. (2022)

Acknowledgments

LARRY RANDOLPH

To my Abba, Father: Many years ago, before I ever heard your "small whisper" that warm August morning, you already had this book planned. I promised then that I would trust and obey your wishes, and you have blessed me beyond my wildest imagination. Each step I have taken over the years has been guided by you, and I am humbled and honored to give you all the glory and praise. Because of your faithfulness, Father, thousands of people—perhaps even millions—have been touched with your message of love, hope, and kindness through our beloved canines and faithful volunteers. I pray this book will touch the hearts of many people and bring them closer to you. I love you.

To Susan, my loving wife and partner in life: You have been with me on this faith journey from the beginning, and it has changed our lives and made us better people. Our walk together with Christ has become stronger through this journey, and I thank you for your thoughtful insights and unwavering devotion. You truly are the "wind beneath my wings" and have made me a better person in more ways than I could have ever thought. I love you now and forever.

To Jen Bleakley: You are a gifted storyteller who is able to weave characters and details in an engaging way. You are a master writer who makes the narrative beautiful and rich, adding details that give every reader a descriptive picture in their mind. Throughout this entire process I often sensed that you knew exactly what my thoughts and words were going to be as you formed and molded them into beautiful phrases throughout this book. Your spiritual heart and love for God has been the foundation of our partnership together. God has given you a special talent, and I am grateful to have been blessed to have you as my coauthor on this journey. Thank you.

To Sarah Atkinson, Carol Traver, Bonne Steffen, and the entire Tyndale team: Sarah, when you reached out to me in late 2021 about this project, you must have believed that my story would be inspiring and encouraging to readers who love dogs and life-changing stories. Thank you for having faith in me to create a book that would bring encouragement and hope to people as they followed this story of faith, obedience, and trust. The entire Tyndale team has been incredibly professional to work with, and I am honored to work with you. Thank you from the bottom of my heart.

To Canines for Christ volunteers: To all the thousands of Canines for Christ volunteers and supporters who have made this book what it is, even though you may not know it. Your faithful service with your beautiful therapy dogs and the powerful stories you have experienced have made this ministry grow and thrive as a testimony to God's message of love and hope to a hurting world. I hope to create in the future a special devotional book with more of these powerful life-changing stories that will encourage and bring joy and hope to many. All of you have made this possible. Thank you.

To my daughters, Kristy, Heather, Brooke, and Tara, my sister Carolyn, and my nine grandchildren. Thank you for your support and encouragement. You have grown up with me in this ministry and have accompanied me on many visits and seen the powerful impact it has had on people. I pray your lives will be enhanced in a greater way through this wonderful ministry and through this book. I am blessed to have all of you in my life, and I love each one of you.

Finally, my sweet and faithful companion and heart dog, Gracie. You, my special girl, were the matriarch and queen of this ministry. Throughout the years you were loyal and unrelenting in visiting thousands of people in hundreds of places throughout the country. Your warm nose, soulful eyes, and wagging tail brought enormous joy and comfort to countless numbers of people who opened their hearts to you. Thank you for opening the door that allowed me to bring God's love, kindness, and powerful message of hope to lost and hurting people. You truly were the pack leader of thousands of therapy dogs in our ministry, and your legacy will live on throughout history. I love you, my sweet girl. Thank you, God, for giving me your dogs to use to reach many people in your name.

JENNIFER MARSHALL BLEAKLEY

Larry and Susan, I will forever be grateful to God for allowing me to meet you guys. You have become like family, and I will always treasure our friendship. Thank you for trusting me with your story.

Sweet Gracie, you truly were the Canines for Christ queen. Thank you for pointing so many people's hearts to Jesus. And

Sadie, thank you for snuggling with me on the sofa when Sarah and I came to visit. You were born to touch people's hearts—just like you did mine that day!

Steve Kesler, thank you so much for allowing me to shadow you at the beginning of this project. You are a ray of light in this world and are clearly doing what God put you on this earth to do.

Laura Stewart, thank you for allowing me to share a little bit of your story, and for patiently answering my questions and sending me photos of your beautiful dogs. You are such a gift!

To every Canines for Christ volunteer, chaplain, junior volunteer, supporter, and dog, thank you for the work you do. God is working through you all in beautiful and powerful ways.

To my incredible Tyndale Team—

Sarah Atkinson, I can never thank you enough for trusting me with this project. Thanks for making the trip with me to Tampa—and for always being a safe place for me to land.

Bonne Steffen, thank you for being such an incredible editor and friend. You are an absolute joy to work with.

Carol Traver, thank you for lending your storytelling genius to this project—and for sending me sacred pine cones and quokka photos to keep me going!

Alyssa Clements, Annette Hayward, Libby Dykstra, Brianna Coyle, Megan Alexander, and Mary Mayo, thank you for everything you did to bring this book to life and into people's hands. I am so thankful for each and every one of you.

Dave Schroeder, I am so grateful to get to work with you. Thanks for always being there and for always having an awesome animal story to share!

Mom and Daddy and Aunt Judy, thank you for all the prayers and encouragement—and for your constant belief in me.

A big thank you to my friends and family for being there in such sweet and practical ways while I worked on this book. I am so grateful for your friendship and presence in my life.

Darrell, you are my home and my safe place. Thank you for always being there and for always believing in me.

Andrew, you are one of the bravest, smartest, kindest, and most awesome people I know. I am so proud to be your mom. Keep looking up, buddy!

Ella, you are one of the wisest, most creative, thoughtful, and amazing people I know. I am so honored to be your mom. Keep your face toward the light, sweet girl!

Jesus, you are my constant, my strength, my steady, my hope. May the words of this book honor you, and may your love and light shine through its pages.

And finally, I'd like to say a big thank you to those who train and work with therapy dogs. Your work is sacred and important, and you are impacting so many lives. Thank you!

About the Authors

Larry Randolph is the founder of Canines for Christ, a board-certified crisis response chaplain, and a Billy Graham rapid response chaplain. Since beginning Canines for Christ in 2007 with his wife, Susan, Larry has seen the therapy dog program grow into an international volunteer-based ministry reaching hundreds of thousands of people with God's love. The couple live in Tampa, Florida, with their English Labrador Retriever, Sadie, and are parents to four children and grandparents to nine.

Jennifer Marshall Bleakley is author of *Joey* and *Project Solomon*, as well as the Pawverbs devotional series. She has worked as a child and family grief counselor and holds a master's degree in mental health counseling from Nova Southeastern University. She lives in Raleigh, North Carolina, with her husband, Darrell, their two children, and a menagerie of pets.

Canines 4 Christ

Canines for Christ Therapy Dog Ministry, Inc., seeks to shine the love of Christ through our volunteers and our canines as his disciples. We provide a ministry of presence that actively engages with people who need the compassion that only God's message can provide.

Our canines and volunteers serve in hospitals, 911 call centers, special-needs facilities, courtrooms, crisis response situations, nursing homes, police and fire departments, schools, hospice centers, cancer centers, and other places of need. As a Christian-based therapy dog ministry, we use ordinary people and their beloved dogs to share God's powerful message of love and hope to communities throughout our country and world.

For more information, please contact us at canines4christ.org or

Chaplain Jill Powell
jill@canines4christ.org
877-409-3009
Canines for Christ, P.O. Box 28, Lutz, FL 33548

Heartwarming tales of real-life pets, combined with inspiring truths about *love, devotion, and faith* from the book of Proverbs

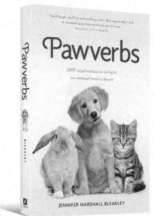

A heartwarming true story of

LOYALTY, KINDNESS & HEALING,

Joey is a profound testament to the power of blind faith.

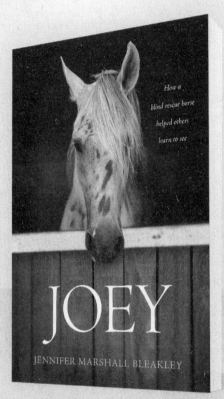

When a struggling ranch owner dedicated to helping troubled
kids rescues a blind horse named Joey, the result is a story of
friendship, faith, and overcoming. *Joey* will touch your heart and
reveal the power of finding light in the darkest of places.